F-BOMB YOUR LIFE

An Incomplete Guide to
Totally Screwing up
Everything

GREGORY SCOTT KASE

Copyright © 2013 Gregory Scott Kase

King Kong Fuzi Publishing

All rights reserved. No part of this book may be used or reproduced in any manner whatsoever without written permission from the author except in the case of brief quotations embodied in critical articles and reviews. For permission requests, write to the publisher, addressed "Attention: Permissions Coordinator," at the address below: kingkongfuzi@yahoo.com.

Publisher's Note: This is a work of opinion. Names, characters, places, and incidents are either a product of the author's imagination or have been changed to protect people's privacy. It is the author's intent to provide general information in an effort to help you better your life. Should you act upon your constitutional right to use anything in this book for yourself, the author and the publisher assume no responsibility for your actions.

F-Bomb Your Life/Gregory Scott Kase — 1st ed.
ISBN: 978-0615761534

This book is dedicated to those who seek.

CONTENTS

Acknowledgments		ix
Introduction		1
Part 1: The Fun Years		5
1	**How to F-bomb Your Love Life**	7
	Intro	7
	Just Be Yourself	8
	Put a Price on Everything	12
	Trust Your Gut	16
	Glorify the Past	20
	Go Back to the Future	23
	Get Your Groove On	26
2	**How to F-bomb Your Finances**	31
	Intro	31
	Don't Save for Retirement (or Anything Really)	31

	Spend Money Like You Have It	35
	Go Big Ticket Now	40
	Don't Research Before You Buy	45
	Buy Everything You Don't Need	47
3	**How to F-bomb Your Education**	53
	Intro	53
	Go It Alone	54
	Sleep In	58
	Do It Tomorrow	60
	Get a Hobby	63
4	**How to F-bomb Your Social Life**	67
	Intro	67
	Cover Your Spread	68
	Blend In	71
	Tell It Like It Is	74
	Look Out for Numero Uno	76

Part 2: The Other Years ... 81

5 **How to F-bomb Your Marriage** ... 83
   Intro ... 83
   Always Be Right ... 85
   Never Argue ... 88
   Refuse to Listen ... 92
   Divide and Conquer ... 95
   Be Somewhere Else ... 100

6 **How to F-bomb Your Career** ... 105
   Intro ... 105
   Take It Personally ... 106
   Keep It to Yourself ... 109
   Keep It Fair ... 112

7 **How to F-bomb Your Health** ... 117
   Intro ... 117
   Don't Rest for Nuthin' ... 118
   Rush Right In ... 120
   Go Get Your Fast Food Fix ... 122

	Live for Moderation	124
	Swim in Denial River	126
8	**How to F-bomb Your Family**	131
	Intro	131
	Abuse Substance	132
	Fret About It	134
	Get Your Glow Tan On	136
	Fahgetta Bout It	139
9	**How to F-bomb Your Religion**	143
	Intro	143
	Just Sit Back and Listen	144
	Straddle that Fence	146
	Heal Thyself	147
	Tell a Story	148
	Play for the Other Team	149
	Rest on Your Laurels	150
	In Closing	153
	About the Author	155

ACKNOWLEDGMENTS

I'd like to thank all those who shared their stories for this project. It is great fun living through others, but you know how I so love getting in the muck myself. And I am indebted to my family and friends who supported me while writing this, even though you all advised to "never lower yourself to such pursuits." This of course propelled me to write the book in the first place, as I'm far removed from good advice.

I would also like to thank those test readers who suffered through first drafts and final ones. Your enthusiasm and love for "telling me like it is" is such a vital part of my creative process. I am most grateful.

And lastly, I'd like to thank my son, Rex, for the inspired art work, which is brilliant in its simplicity. I learn much from you, Son, and your advice I will gladly take for the rest of my days.

INTRODUCTION

Have you ever asked for advice and then did the exact opposite of what you were told? Yeah, me too. All the time. But why do we do this? Over and over again. Is it because we don't like the advice we get? Or could it be that we're too impatient to do things the *right* way?

I know for me, it's a little of both . . . and because I think I'm so much smarter than most of the dimwits giving out that free advice. I rationalize that a good deal of luck must have been involved with their success, as it seems that on any given day, most of them couldn't find their way out of the ball pit at McDonald's. And I'm supposed to take advice from them? No thanks.

Now have you ever had things blow up in your face after you didn't take someone's advice? Yeah, me too. All the time. What the heck? Why do I not take *that* advice—the advice that just may keep all my man parts where they were meant to be?

INTRODUCTION

While using big words like *pontificating* to search for my answers, it hit me square in the jimmy—my son's fastball that is. I was quickly reminded that the old "keep your eye on the ball" advice did indeed have merit, as does other advice out there. But for some reason, I don't heed most advice. So I asked myself two things: Do I *really* want to get things right? And where in the hell did that fastball come from?

Since I blatantly ignore life's "good" advice, do I actually have some deep-seated fear of success? I know it's not a fear of failure because I'm a little too good at that. And if it is truly some warped fear of success, then I can't be alone on this because I know too many people who suck at life just as much as I do.

And then it hit me—not another fastball, but an honest-to-God idea. Why not finally give the world a book that caters to this concept of not *really* wanting to get things right? Why not show all the poor souls like me how best to "get it wrong," and maybe even have some fun along the way? And while we're at it, why not take some of that "good" advice we all get and show how sometimes even the best advice is not so sound in the wrong hands?

I call this approach "F-bombing your life," and it embraces our fear of success. Think of it as your chance to finally take some advice and run with it. And if you don't, you just may be forced to deal with that closet demon called Success; just saying his name gives me the willies!

INTRODUCTION

To slay this wicked demon, I have brought forth many methods that have totally screwed up my life in some unforgivable way. And I've even consulted other people who've made it their lifelong mission to never take good advice and to instead do their own thing. They've shared their stories with me and have even helped to highlight a few of my own. So some of the stories in this book are theirs, but admittedly, most are my own.

I must say, however, that the stories in this book are all "almost true" (lawyer-speak for 'figments of the author's imagination that in no way could be used to sue said author for leaking said events in a public forum'). And while it's "all true" that these events have F-bombed quite a few lives, it should be understood that there are many ways to ruin your life, countless ways if I'm to be so bold. Thus, this work is not meant to be all-inclusive, as that would be damned near impossible . . . and incredibly taxing.

Thus, I've tried to cover only the more modern methods of F-bombing, especially since it has been around since Adam and Eve. Yeah, remember that story?

Eve: Look at that pretty, red apple!
Adam: If you're hungry, go get some of that low, hanging fruit.
Eve: I *want* that apple!
Adam: C'mon, man! You already got one of my ribs; isn't that enough? Besides, the only advice we got was to leave the apples alone.

INTRODUCTION

Eve: Okay then; I'll just talk to you all night instead. I've got so many decorating ideas—
Adam: Fine! But if I scratch my beans climbing that tree, you'll be playing doctor . . .

And so the first F-bomb was born (apparently I'm related to Adam). As is evident from Adam's story, or the fact that we actually know his story, our culture has a long-standing fascination with storytelling. So it's my hope that you'll share what you learn from this book (along with some of your own "What did I just do?" moments). I also hope you'll review this book on whatever site from which you bought / borrowed / stole it. Reviewing is one of the only ways we can truly express our voices and be heard by the world . . . that and writing how-to books.

One final thing, and a warning at that: some or all of the sections in this book may make you spew like Old Faithful. Why? Because maybe you attempted to read too many sections in one sitting, and deep down, you can't handle all the destruction. Or maybe you pick things up faster than others and don't need so many examples. Or maybe you object to the use of so many F-bombs. So if any part of this book makes you a little queasy, and you haven't just eaten something you know you shouldn't have eaten, put the book down, take a deep breath, and try to relax. Then resume reading when you have the stomach for it. And if it's the writing, just keep that to yourself.

PART 1: THE FUN YEARS

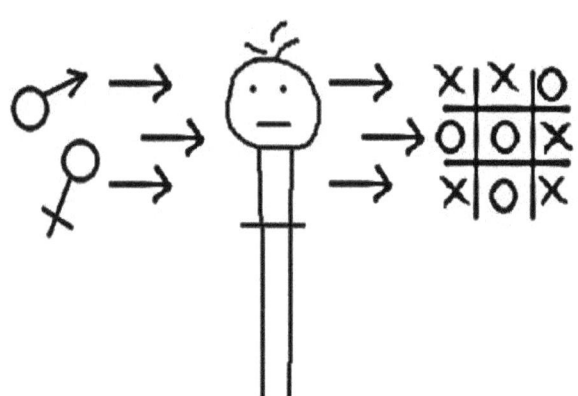

1

HOW TO F-BOMB YOUR LOVE LIFE

Intro

My love life, like most, has been rife with that stomach-churning, giddy stuff that leads to the well of stupidity. And boy do I drink up! But I've realized that most of the things born from that well are actually F-bombs in disguise. As a silver lining though, my love-life stupidity turned out to be a good thing for all my single friends, because when they didn't have a love life, they sure as hell didn't want me to have one either.

So please pay particular attention to this section, as it just may give you what you need to save those friendships . . . you know, the ones you forget about when you find someone to swap spit with and the ones you run back to when that spit gives you "cold sores." And don't worry, no matter how deeply you're in love, a few well-timed F-bombs will take care of everything.

If you don't believe in love, then congratulations; you don't even have to read this chapter. You get a pass on this one, and that will put an extra ten minutes back into your day. Now go cuddle with all those cats and think about which chapter you want to read next.

Just Be Yourself

Everyone always told me to just be myself, and this makes me wonder if they were secretly wishing for me to fail. It's not like I was some tall, dark, and handsome stud-muffin with so much to offer (I was more of a pasty, warped tic tac). The only thing I had to offer was myself as a sacrifice, taking the girl who no one else wanted but who came with the group package.

After spending years as the proverbial jackass wingman, I finally came to the conclusion that all my friends actually wanted me to be single forever. "Just be yourself," they said. After all, it's who I'd been my whole life. But it turns out that *Just Be Yourself* is a common refrain because, quite frankly, people don't know what else to say, or rather they do know but don't want to say. These "friends" of mine knew me better than anyone, being all too familiar with my idiosyncrasies (those which repelled XX chromosomes faster than Pee Wee Herman in a thong). Yet I still got this *awesome* advice, and each time I followed it, I took a step closer to becoming that 40-year-old down the street who still lives with his mother.

Ask anyone who has made it to the big show (marriage), and they'll tell you that they weren't exactly themselves all the time. Why? Because *Just Be Yourself* puts you back on the one-lane road to nowhere. This is advice you can count on. Take it from me, I spent most of my life just being myself, a.k.a. being single. When I ditched *Just Be Yourself* I ended up with a ring on my finger. How's that for solid proof?

But wait, you may be thinking, *maybe you hadn't met the right girl yet*. And if you just thought that, then you have fallen into a trap with sharper teeth than *Just Be Yourself*. That "right one yet" BS was nothing but one more excuse uttered to make me feel good about myself after yet another girl mysteriously said "no thanks."

To make matters worse, it's something my *mother* would say. I don't know about you, but I outgrew the "right one yet" speech at age ten. Yes, I very much liked girls at that age, and no, they did not like me so much. And back then, I knew no other way than *Just Be Yourself*—further proof that this stuff works.

Just being yourself may wreck your love life, but you can have fun with it too. No longer do you have to worry about what your date will think. Just got back from yoga class and there's still a little gas left in the tank? Let 'er rip. Just slammed that beer to prove you can hang with the boys? Release that thunderous stench. The point is to just be yourself.

This reckless abandon of just being yourself means something different to everyone. So don't force the examples I've given if that's not you. You could actually end up with the opposite effect and draw your lover into your arms forever. So keep it real, and just be yourself.

And one note of caution: while it's true that on extremely rare occasions just being yourself leads to everlasting love, please don't concern yourself with such fantasy. That elusive pipedream of eternal love only happens when *both* people are just being themselves. And that's about as likely as Cupid shooting Larry Flynt and Ellen DeGeneres with the same arrow.

Here's an *almost true* story by/about a real-life F-bomber to hammer it home.

Let's change my name to Depardieu because it rhymes with 'in plain view.' Depardieu was a good soul. I helped old ladies cross the street, I played bingo at the country club, and I had an amazing stamp collection. An all-around good guy I was. And then one day while eating at the food court in the mall, I saw this wild stallion of a man dump his teriyaki chicken in the trash along with the girl next to him. Tears flowed down her face, leaving behind the cutest little zebra pattern of cheap eyeliner and ghostly foundation.

As stallion boy left the stable, I, being the good soul that I was, thought I would go over and cheer the girl up. I thought about all the cool one-liners I'd seen in the movies and even envisioned myself sweeping in to save the day. I gathered my courage and sauntered over to the filly, and right before I opened my mouth, I heard a little voice whisper, "Just be yourself." And being the good soul that I was, I listened.

I disposed of the rough and tough demeanor that I had seen in the movies, the one that would've had me kicking one chair out of the way, grabbing another to spin around so that I could hang over the back of it, and saying something like, "You okay babe?" Instead I opted for a softer approach, one that was more like me. So I timidly asked if the seat next to this weeping willow was taken and then apologized for the way that Man Stallion had treated her.

Her response? "Get away from me, you freak!" And I did, because I was just being myself.

I, Depardieu, F-bombed my love life by just being myself. But I was a dork you may say. No, I was just being myself. And no matter how together you think you are, you will Depardieu yourself if you too *Just Be Yourself*. This is dangerous. It's like comparing that girl to a filly in one sentence and then changing her into a tree in the next. You just don't do crap like that if you want to write good stuff, but I had to because that's what happens with this technique. You go from being frisky and curious to a block of wood with bark skin. I might as well have been a hardwood floor so that people could have walked all over me. This is F-bombing, so get out there and *Just Be Yourself!*

Put a Price on Everything

Money, money, money! Nothing gets someone's attention like money does. Mo' money, no money, it doesn't matter. Some of us use money, and for some, money uses us. But we all have a relationship with it. So why not bring money right through the front door of that budding love life?

As a guy, I always wanted to know if a girl I liked had a job, so I could ensure that her accessories wouldn't eat into the proverbial beer budget. And girls were always interested in how much money I made to ensure that I at least had something going for me. But finding out these answers and more (without it being naked-old-man awkward) is hard to do in most cases. But not to worry. We're going to *Put a Price on Everything*, because there's nothing quite like someone who nickels and dimes a conversation to death. And this works whether you're Ms. Money Bags or Mr. Dirty Rags.

The beauty of this technique is that it doesn't take any extra study or hard work on our part. Our minds have been programmed to remember how much things cost. For example, I've gone to the grocery store, filled my cart up to the brim, proceeded through the checkout line, and then suddenly said, "Uh, those apples were four for a dollar." That's pretty incredible given that I can go to a party, be introduced to one person, and forget her name twenty seconds later. If her name had been Two-bit-Twit or Dollar-Installer, I'd never forget her or her name. Why? 'Cause I just put a price on her.

Here's how it works. Next time you're on a date, talk about how much money you make, how much money you just paid for the kicks on your feet, how much money the dinner's gonna be, etc. And if talking like this embarrasses you, this technique may not be the one for you. It has made many a first date my last date, though, so I know it works. And it even works to get rid of all the losers your "friends" set you up with . . . because you two had so much in common.

If the rich money talk feels insincere because you simply don't have any money, don't fret! I've gone my whole life without much money. You can still put a spin on this technique to make it work for you. Remember when I said that this method works for Ms. Money Bags or Mr. Dirty Rags? Well, this is the dirty rags part. There's even a fancy term for it—poor-mouthing. It's old school, and like it sounds, it lets everyone know how much money you *don't* have. And it can reach a deeper level than the braggart (a.k.a. blow-hard) way of telling just how much you *do* have, as it has a modest bent.

Here's an example of how it has worked for me. My date: "What's wrong?" Me: "I can't pay my electric bill because I got a pay cut at work, and now my great uncle won't be getting his lung transplant because I had been keeping the good lung in my freezer for him, and it thawed out along with my favorite ice cream which I only ate so that I wouldn't pick up smoking and end up like my great uncle." My date: "$?#@&!"

Do you see the poor-mouthing difference? In a bizarre way, I was begging for sympathy by putting a price on everything, and I never even had to say it out loud. I let my prices (hardship) go to work for me. As you can imagine, this made my dates question way more about me than they ever intended. This method also works to get rid of someone who you know deep down is just not that into you.

Sometimes I started with a variety of F-bombs tailor-made for my love life, but for some reason, they didn't detonate. Putting a price on everything was often the trigger I needed to blow the hell out of my situation. So be cheap or overindulgent. Just make sure you talk about it on your dates.

And if the person you're dating is still on you like yesterday's BO, then they're probably after your money. And since this is the only person who is actually staying with you, you will most likely marry this lucky individual. At that point, read the chapter on how to F-bomb your marriage and make sure you follow it precisely. If that still doesn't work, you are one wealthy son of a bitch and need to start sending me a few checks to spread some of that misfortune around.

Here's another *almost true* story by/about a real-life F-bomber to hammer it home.

We will call her Flo Honey because it rhymes with 'mo' money.' Flo Honey was a stripper, or at least she wanted to be because she liked having men fawn over her and give her all their money. So one day while she was cutting hair, she met a man who drove up in a shiny, new Mercedes (I am neither the driver nor the stripper in this story by the way). He had his hair slicked back, and he strangely resembled a full-bellied toad. Flo Honey thought this amphibian was quite interesting. He spoke of all the places he'd been, all the people he'd met, all the charities he'd given money to, and all the expensive places that he wanted to take her.

Flo Honey liked this, so she agreed to go out with Toady. And true to his word, he took her to all the expensive places and even bought her many expensive things. It did not take long for Flo Honey to figure out that this was a healthy arrangement. In a few months' time, Flo Honey decided to move on over to Toady's pad.

It was a storybook setting. But every day, Toady talked about the same thing—money. And although the topics of conversation were different, they all made their way back to Toady and his money. This began to bore Flo Honey. And she became frustrated because no matter how many times she kissed Toady, he remained the same wart of a man.

All of a sudden, Toady was not being loved anymore. Toady couldn't understand. But what about his money? What about his brilliant conversation? F-bombs were flying and they weren't even made of money! Toady got upset and kicked Flo Honey off his pad. But why? Flo Honey was still naturally sweet. But I guess when you have all that money, you just have no room for Flo Honey.

I never liked Toady. He was an arrogant ass, much like myself when I decided to *not* be myself and get the girl. But Toady was a good F-bomber. So I should respect him for that I guess. And Toady is still single, which keeps my faith in this manner of F-bombing your love life. Who says you can't put a price on love?

Trust Your Gut

This is another one of those words-of-wisdom moments. "Trust your gut" is often the casual answer to statements like "Do you think she's the one?" Trust your gut? As if I could digest this love stuff on my own? I'm sorry, but this is more of that advice that I just don't get . . . unless my friends were secretly trying to sabotage my happiness, which as we've already discussed is a real possibility.

"Trust your gut" is a caveman term because it is primitive and should only be used for the art of survival. Cave people once sat around pondering life's mysteries. Will fire melt my face? Do saber-toothed tigers make good pets? Is this nail fungus edible? To them, these were flip-a-coin decisions. They either got it right or they got it wrong. Cave people who were wrong often died in the moment. The ones who were always right had better guts. Hence, "trust your gut" was born.

"Trusting your gut" is absurdly comical if you're looking for success at love. I was still single all those years for a reason. I relied on that gut of mine for far too long. Shouldn't I have trusted someone else's gut if I wanted love? Like someone who'd been married four or five times? At least they would've had a proven track record of getting back to the big show.

What's funny (to me anyway) is that some people know better than to trust their own gut, yet they go and seek solace from one of their single friends. See the irony in this? They could be going straight to a skilled artisan in love life F-bombing, and would have been if they ever came to me. Hilarious, don't you think?

If you put a little slant on it and believe in yourself a little too much, "Trusting your gut" can also lead to thinking "I know best." I know the best places to go. I know the best ways to get results in the gym. I know the best ways to properly install the toilet paper. Essentially, I know it all (my dates came to rue the day my gut was born). So, whether you've got a big gut or you're all butt, this is a sound approach, and it almost always ensures that you will be single forever.

Here's another *almost true* story by/about a real-life F-bomber to hammer it home.

Let's change my name to Larry because it rhymes with 'contrary.' Larry was sitting around with his buddy one day talking about a girl he had just met. I told Buddy how I met this girl at a club, and how we danced all night together. And how we shared longing glances and almost a momentary kiss before she excused herself to go to the ladies room. While I was waiting for her return, I looked at my watch and knew two things: one, I should have been home hours ago, and two, the club was about to close. Sure enough, right then, someone turned on the bright lights and cut the music.
I stood there blinded by the light, inching along in a mass of people toward the door. My new friend was nowhere to be seen. I looked around, but she had vanished. Where did she go? I even asked another girl to go into the ladies room to see if anyone was left. Nobody. I was saddened by this discovery. Now I would have to go home alone.

As I walked to my car, I heard the clickety-clack of high heels getting louder behind me. I turned to look, and it was the girl's friend. She handed me a fragment of torn napkin with the words "call me" scrawled on it. And as the girl ran away, she mouthed how much her friend liked me. This made my night, and this new-found enthusiasm for life carried over into the next day when I met up with Buddy.

"So what do you think?" I said.
"I don't like it."
"What? You're crazy!" I said to Buddy, who was happily married and never spent a night alone even when he was single.
"Okay, what are you going to do?" Buddy asked.
"I don't know, what do you think I should do?"
"I think you should call this girl in a few days and ask her out for coffee."
"I don't know, Buddy. A girl like this won't be around in a few days. She could have any guy she wanted."
"No offense, bro, but why would she go for you?"
"Dude! I'm more of a ladies man now that I've come into my own."
"What does that even mean?" Buddy asked.
"Look dude, I'm calling her today."
"Is that what you're gut's tellin' ya?"
"Watch and learn, be-otch!"
I dialed the phone. "Hi, can I please speak to Mandie?"
Voice on other line said, "Hold on, I'll get him."

This is what happens when single people

trust their guts. Buddy's gut was telling him that I was about to get my ass kicked by this girl's boyfriend or that she didn't want to be seen outside the black lights of the club for a reason. Of course not even Buddy predicted what had happened next, but he did get a good laugh over it and used it to make sure that I would stay single for far longer than he ever anticipated. Everyone who knows this story still wonders what would have happened if the club would have been open a little longer. Now that would have been a story!

Glorify the Past

This is one of my favorites because everyone likes to share stories, or at least I do. And where do these stories come from? Our past of course. And I've figured out that these stories define who we are, telling us where we've been and illustrating where we'll probably never go.

It was hard for my ancient stories to tell me where I was going in my love life because *nowhere* is not actually a place. It is the absence of location or direction, which is precisely where my love life was after sharing all my stories. It turns out that my life, no matter how riveting to me, is cancelled-sitcom boring to the rest of the world. Bottom line: if my date wasn't a big part of those stories, I, along with those stories, got old quickly.

To take this method a step further, it was always an awesome dating adventure when I brought along my ex for a ride down memory lane. I'm not talking about physically bringing my ex on the date with me. That would've been too much of a hassle, what with scheduling availability and deciding who's going to pay for what when the bill came. No, it was easier than that. All I had to do was bring my ex up in conversation—in any context. That's it. And the more instances I brought up my ex, the deeper the hole I dug. My love life never had a chance.

With this ploy, you can go all negative Nelly and say how your ex was such an idiot and could never do anything right, or you can say how really wonderful she was, but that she just wasn't right for you. Either way, you will be on your way to F-bombing your love life. Talk badly about your ex, and apparently you're labeled as hard to please. Talk nicely about your ex, and you're labeled as even harder to please. Strangely, it's a win-win for hosing your love life!

Glorifying the past also sent another hidden message to my partner. For me, living in the past somehow showed that I had no future. It's related to the old adage: "What have you done for me lately." Chances were that I'd done nothing of significance, and glorifying the past only served that up for dessert. And boy was it sweet—love-life-decaying sweet.

Here's another *almost true* story by/about a real-life F-bomber to hammer it home.

We will call him Grover because it rhymes with 'over.' Grover is a very attractive man (your first clue that this is not me). He has a few kids, all still young and living under his roof. And that is a really big roof. Grover has a lot of money. Grover was married, but Mrs. Grover fancied other men and even paid these men for their services. Grover let the first instance go, but others piled up leading him straight into the arms of divorce. Now Mrs. Grover is just another miss. And Grover is back on the market, with a lot to offer by the way.

But strangely, each new person doesn't last long. Grover has been quite intimate with a few, so that doesn't seem to be the problem. So what can it be? Could it be that Grover is glorifying the past? Hmm.

As an experiment, Grover decided to have me go undercover and listen in on his dinner date. So he picked a restaurant with tight seating and made sure I was at the table next to his.

The first five minutes were a sickening love-fest of giggling, eye contact, and graceful touching. But then, the F-bombs were released, and all of a sudden, his date was glaring off into a future that did not include Grover. "My ex picked up the kids tonight." That's how it started. And "Did you enjoy your meal?" is how Grover thought it ended. But it really ended with "My ex picked up the kids tonight."

It was in that moment that her hand casually withdrew from his. It was slight, but that's all it takes. And believe me, it can take a lot less for some (that would be me). So instead of living by "if they don't ask, don't tell," Grover glorified the past, and brought his ex up in conversation.

Those who glorify the past, live in the past, and so they are never removed from the past (which likely never included their dates). And before they know it, their love lives are over just like their past. So for those of you who want to F-bomb your love life, glorify the past, and please don't leave out all the juicy details. Now if you must, go forth and reanimate the past, Dr. Frankenshrine.

Go Back to the Future

We've discussed the benefits of going back to the past, so why not *Go Back to the Future*? We've all seen the movies, and if you haven't, then I suggest you go rent the trilogy. The movies show that when you go back to the future, terrible consequences often result.

There are of course a few layers to this technique. The obvious one to most people, especially after having just read *Glorify the Past*, is that when you focus on the future, it is in essence dissing the present. It is like saying that the present is such a yawn, i.e. your current date is such a yawn. It's bizarre, but just trust me on this one.

One thing I never stopped to consider when I was dating was that talking about the future shined a big spotlight on all the things I hadn't done yet (and that'd be a pretty long list). And even if I was smart enough to include my date in that future, I usually only got creepy looks. Society goes a step further to reinforce this brand of dissing the present every January first by making us proclaim what we're going to do in the coming year. And how have all those New Year resolutions worked out for you? Exactly!

But wait there's more! Going back to the future has another connotation. This part of the plan has us acting like we're *already* in the future. That's right, we act as if the future is now! Let's say I had been dating someone for a few weeks. Of course it's getting pretty serious, so I'd have to make some important decisions like: Is it time to meet the parents? And is it appropriate to discuss nagging infections? Well, the answer is a resounding yes on all counts! A few weeks might as well be an eternity, so it'd be time to let loose. We'd be practically married, and as such, nothing should be off limits. There is no such thing as too much information in a healthy relationship, right? So get on back to the future, because it will help guarantee that you and that lover will have no future.

Here's another *almost true* story by/about a

real-life F-bomber to hammer it home.

We will call her Gwynn because it rhymes with 'rush in.' Gwynn's a talker. She's one of those people you invite to a dinner party because you know that with her around, there will never be a deadly lull in conversation. But the problem is that you can't zone out even for a second because Gwynn is likely to be well into next week.

Gwynn is single. I think that part is a given. And you have to wonder if Gwynn enjoys being single because she is so good at it. Gwynn has no filter either, which makes conversation and everything else that much more entertaining.

Well one night while we were at a concert, Gwynn cheered from the front row. And being so close to the stage, the band's guitarist got a very good look at the vivacious Gwynn. After the concert, Guitar Boy said that he would find her in the bar at the adjacent hotel where we were all staying.

So later on, I see Guitar Boy looking for Gwynn, but Gwynn was already at the bar drinking with another man—one old enough to be her father's grandfather. She talked about all the things she wanted to do with her life and then, in an instant, she took those few minutes with that old raisin and turned them into years down the road. Before I knew it, Gwynn disappeared up the elevator with Wrinkles.

This love connection, if indeed that's what

this was, didn't last though. I think it was because she used this technique of going back to the future. But then he could have used the technique of "putting a price on everything." Given his age, he may have had a mental lapse, and with Gwynn already ten years down the road, thoughts of inflation might have scared Wrinkles nearly to death. Either way, no love blossomed that night.

Get Your Groove On

This is such a basic principle that it almost didn't make the collection. To me, it's like saying "go have an affair." Yes, blatantly obvious to everyone. But I got to thinking that there still may be a few good-hearted souls, just being themselves, who don't realize the power of getting your groove on. So for those few, this one is for you.

You may associate getting your groove on with bringing out your inner Macarena. And while doing so will definitely show that most of us are not suitable for extending the species, this is not what I'm referring to. When I say "get your groove on," I am merely speaking to your being a creature of habit. So it requires no additional training or video dance games, and it is even hard-wired into our DNA.

Think of this as staying in a rut or pattern. Take me for instance. I have thousands of actions that I perform every single day without realizing it. These patterns, which are actually human nature, demonstrate that I lack creativity and am not adventurous. And wouldn't you know it, these traits just happen to be the qualities lovers look for when trying to find a mate. So you see? It's as if I am set up for failure.

Another layer of *Get Your Groove On* is dating the same person over and over and over—not physically the same person, but people just like that person. I used to see this all the time in school. Hot girl dates only "her type," and hot girl then cries her eyes out after "her type" dumps her for "his type," who turns out to be just like her. Cycle then repeats until all the hot girls in town are blind.

This method is good for F-bombing your love life because you have built-in proof that a certain type of person isn't getting your groove. If you're a vegetarian, then by all means keep dating those butchers. I learned long ago that mixing soy beans and beef is the very nature of F-bombing.

Here's another *almost true* story by/about a real-life F-bomber to hammer it home.

Let's change my name to Eugene because it rhymes with 'routine.' Eugene loves a certain dish at a local Thai establishment so much that he refuses to order anything else. It was the first dish I ever tried there, but it was a winner, so I kept it. Perhaps I was secretly hoping the restaurant would rename the dish after me and put my picture on the wall right next to Buddha. And when it came to date night, which strangely did not come around too often, I always suggested the Thai place, even if I had the luxury of a second or third date with the same woman.

Well, I was doing everything right to F-bomb my love life. But the girl I was with on this particular evening was a bit of a wildflower. She did not like routine! As we sat down, she asked me what I always ordered. Of course I told her. But when the waitress came over, my date ordered something else for both of us and then quickly sent the waitress away.

I panicked, but the young spark plug convinced me with her charm and enthusiasm to just let it go. She was getting me to loosen up and live a little. It was very exciting to her, and this strangely excited me. So once our food came, my date kept me engaged by taking a bite and then raving about how good it was with a few expressions that I really wanted to see later on that evening. She then took her fork, loaded it up, and airplaned it right down my hatch (with no fear of getting my germs). This was new and I loved the whole experience.

We quickly ate and headed back to my place. But on the way home, I felt a rush of heat overtake me. Then I felt cold and clammy. Then my stomach protested with whale bellowing. I stepped on the accelerator. Eggplant! One of the dishes must have had eggplant!

My body does not like eggplant. And when we got home, that girl did not like my body! Poor Eugene. I was blinded by beauty (and the fact that a girl was not repulsed by me), causing me to go all crazy and do things like fighting my true F-bombing ways. Had I just kept in my groove, my intestinal fortitude would have stayed intact.

Now it could be said that had I stayed in my groove, I would not have had a chance with that fiery young woman. But you have to ask yourself whether or not I really had a chance with her anyway. So please avoid a trip to the clinic, and just get your groove on. And no matter what *Get Your Groove On* means to you, I am sure that if you follow through with it, the F-bombs will start to fly.

Finances

2

HOW TO F-BOMB YOUR FINANCES

Intro

F-bombing your finances is one of my favorite topics because it is so easy to do . . . and because my family is so good at it. When it comes to finances, I've noticed two types of F-bombers out there: the "aware" F-bomber and the "in-the-dark" F-bomber. Read on to see which camp you're in.

Don't Save for Retirement (or Anything Really)

This is a classic way to F-bomb our finances, and so many of us do it because we want our money now instead of when we're old and feeble. And it is very easy to get lost in the logic of how things like a 401k plan could actually be a good thing, which makes F-bombing that much easier. For instance, when I got my first real job, the "people at work" said I needed to invest in the 401k plan, but to someone who didn't have a quarter for the gumball machine, the 401k smelled fishy, or as my kid would say, it "smelled like yoga."

The premise was simple: pay the 401k now in hopes of it paying me later (like in fifty years). And I didn't even know whether mac-n-cheese could sustain me for that long. In the financial sector, this is called risk. And risk is scary. I thought that all of that hard-earned money I made while pixel-watching could have gone into a 401k, which would have then be used only to later pay for unclogging my cheese-filled arteries. Would it not be better for me to just get my money now and eat a decent meal?

Some of my friends went with the 401k early on and now have a crap load of money. They plan to retire in a few years and get their money later. I am of course waiting for their impending heart attacks so that I can give them that "I told you so" look.

And what's to keep the government from passing a new retirement age that has me slobbering all over myself before I can get my *own* money back without paying a penalty? Now that's messed up. And that's why this technique can be so stealth. Not saving for retirement actually has some merit if you twist your logic enough, and boy am I twisted!

Let's face it. I just don't know what my future

holds. I could be a strange statistic up for a Darwin award, or I could live to be old and senile. Either way, there remains the chance that I will not be spending all my money. Since I realized that I will someday need money to buy mac-n-cheese, I'm *now* storing away a few dollars in my 401k for the eventual rainy day. But how pessimistic is it that I would expect rainy days? This makes me want to go find the people who convinced me to do a 401k and give them a titty twister. And don't worry about me giving up on this technique; this is one of those times where "never too late to start" does not apply.

Here's another *almost true* story by/about a real-life F-bomber to hammer it home.

We will call him Gary because it rhymes with 'scary.' Gary is a dear relative of mine who taught me everything I know about never saving a nickel. Anyway, he lived in the moment, giving his family the life he thought they wanted. Gary was a model citizen too, never getting into trouble, eating his vegetables, and respecting everyone around him who shared his views. All in all, a pretty good use of flesh and bone.

In his twenties, Gary was handsome, so he had that going for him. In his thirties, he was well into fatherhood. In his forties, he was still deep into fatherhood. In his fifties, he was still a hard worker out making a living. In his sixties, he was still a pretty good consumer of things. In his seventies, he woke up and realized he had no money, that he was too old to work, and that Social Security was neither social nor offered much security.

"I reached the end of my rope," Gary lamented.
"What about your 401k?" I asked.
"Never started one of those. Besides, we always needed the money."
"It'd be nice to have some of that money now," I said, wondering how long it would take for him to start bumming money from the rest of our financial fugitive family.
"Never knew I'd make it this long. You know people used to die when they hit my age."
"So, what are you going to do?" I asked.
"I'll have to file for bankruptcy."
"Don't worry," I said. "You'll be back in the saddle in another seven years!"
Gary said nothing and walked away.

On the surface, it looks like Gary was able to get a lot of the things he wanted, when he wanted them (in his youth anyway). And it even seems that working into his sixties paid off in a way, as he was able to put more money into the old government kitty. But in the end, not saving for retirement gave him the royal screw. Gary is decimated and ashamed, not knowing whether or not he will soon be on the street with his wife and arthritic dog. Now that's F-bombing at its best!

Spend Money Like You Have It

Sounds fun, right? Well, that's because it is. Who doesn't like to blow a wad of cash? Our culture is built on spending money. It is good for the economy, and it is good for the soul. Have you ever walked into a store and bought exactly what you wanted? I'm talking about skipping the sale rack and throwing down the big bucks. Well, I hope you have because it's euphoric and works for just about anything.

Even if you're the geeked out scientist holed away in a lab somewhere (like I was), you can put down a mere $600 to get the latest and greatest, "I'm so sexy" eyeglasses to really pump up your wow factor. Spending money like this is absolute power. And power is good. But to get it, you may have to let go of the green. Some people are natural tightwads like me (obviously from many years dining on mac-n-cheese and bailing family members out of trouble), but this is something that can be fixed. I'm living proof.

Back in the day, I only bought from the sale racks after going from store to store to make sure I got the very best deal. This not only pissed off my friends when I was the driver, but it was wearing me out and holding me back. Yes, I always got a good deal, but in the process, I looked like yesterday's news. And you know what they say about yesterday's news . . . it lines today's birdcages.

As you can imagine, this was not good for my

single life. As it turned out, while I was trying to be responsible financially, I was totally F-bombing my love life. Now, I spend money like I have it. And it feels good. There really is something to "keeping up with Joneses."

And in this high-tech world that we live in, having yesterday's solution is just not good enough anymore. You have to buy what's now, i.e. what's hip and trendy. It's important to be the one in your group who's always one step ahead of everyone else, especially if you have friends with IBS.

Here's a little test to gauge how well you've got this one down . . .

You just got the iPad-infinity and the next version, iPad-beyond infinity, comes out. Do you:

A) Feel sorry for yourself because you just got the iPad-infinity
B) Complain to all your friends who are getting the latest version
C) Tell everyone there's really no difference between the two versions
D) Get rid of that iPad-infinity like it's bad breath and get what's fresh

If you're like the new me, you're spending money like you have it, and you picked D. It's so obvious. And you know what else? We should have never been in this position to begin with. If we just got the iPad-infinity, why did we wait so long to get it? We should've already had that glass worn down to its circuitry, begging for something else to replace that old, stodgy relic.

See what can be averted when we take a leap of faith and spend all our money? For one, we wouldn't be feeling sorry for ourselves because we would be the envy of all our friends. And we would still have friends because they wouldn't have dumped our sorry butts for complaining all the time. And we wouldn't have to degrade ourselves by lying to cover up our frugality (tightwadiness).

Now I realize that spending money like you have it costs money. And I also realize that most of us aren't professional athletes with million-dollar bling in our grills. The way around this is credit. Even if your credit score is just north of your favorite baseball player's batting average, there will still be some idiot bank out there who will give you a line of credit. I know, right? Call it supporting the world economy with all that spending you'll be doing.

I feel I should caution you to *not* spend too much money so that you can better handle that time of the month . . . when minimum monthly payments come due. This is the time when the old me comes out of hiding and has a panic attack. But after all, you are F-bombing your finances, so why bother? And by the way, you don't have to stop at just one credit card.

And then there's the wonderful world of checks. I know the only people who use checks anymore are little, old ladies in front of you at the check-out line taking twenty minutes to buy antacid. But you can write checks when you don't even have money in your account to cover your purchases. Sounds bizarre, but it's true. And you know what the bank does? Of course you do. They charge a small fee for your poor math skills. A small fee to get what I want, when I want it? No brainer in the F-bomber's world. Now go find out what the latest "must-have" is and *Spend Money Like You Have It*!

Here's another *almost true* story by/about a real-life F-bomber to hammer it home.

Believe it or not, this is actually about another dear family member of mine. Yes, we do know how to F-bomb our finances! We will call her Glenda because it rhymes with 'pretenda.' Glenda is a free spirit if ever there was one. And from an early age, she had this concept of spending money like you have it down pat. If she saw something she wanted, she got it. There was no lay-away, no saving up for it. There was only right now.

And she is so skilled in bouncing checks that you would think she was a financial sumo wrestler. It is a thing of beauty really. She plants one foot at a time in a confident display before charging toward the cash register with her items in hand. She then stares down the cashier, daring her to reject her worthless scribbles. The cashier trembles at the possibility of losing such a big sale for the store before conceding victory to little, old Glenda. I often wonder if the outcome would ever be different if the cashier were to steal a glance of Glenda bumming money for gas in the parking lot.

Me: "Do you really think that's right, knowing you don't have any money?"

Glenda: "I have to have my smokes!" (She zeroes in on the one part of the purchase that feeds her addiction.)

Me: Silence. Still confused.

Glenda: "You know how hard it is to quit these things? And these things are expensive!"

Me: "So it's the tobacco company's fault you have no money?"

Glenda (coughs): "Don't be ridiculous."

Me: "Did you ever go to the doctor about that cough?"

Glenda: "Yeah."

Me: "And?"

Glenda: "I need to take this medicine or I might die."

Me: "What medicine?"

Glenda: "I don't know. The pharmacy won't take my checks for some reason."

Me: "Why don't you just charge it?"

Glenda (coughs): "I got my cards taken a few months ago."

Me: "So what now?"

Glenda: "I'll get disability to pay for it."

It is impressive to me that when Glenda was faced with adversity, she still found a way to have someone pay for her stuff. This is truly a gift, and it is a testament to spending money like you have it. Here is this woman, living her life, spending well beyond her means, and still looking forward to the next purchase. It brings tears to my eyes. F-bomb those finances, Glenda, F-bomb away!

Go Big Ticket Now

Perhaps a subcategory of *Spend Money Like You Have It* is *Go Big Ticket Now*. But you'll soon see why this subcategory gets its very own section. First of all, what does "big ticket" mean? I'm not talking about tickets to the Super Bowl or the World Series, although those are fantastic uses of your money in the F-bomb world, especially if you can't afford them. No, I'm talking about those big purchases we all need in life: cars, boats, homes, appliances, etc. So while the mantra of *Spend Money Like You Have It* relates more to the everyday purchases we make, *Go Big Ticket Now* relates to those things we just don't get to buy every day—the things that truly make us happy and complete.

While it would be nice to buy a new car every year, that's just not going to happen for us F-bombers. And if you could collect cars like they were Hot Wheels, I'm sorry, but chances are you've never F-bombed your finances, nor are you capable of doing so (unless you just came into a crap load of money playing the lottery). But for the rest of us normal denizens of depravity, this section highlights the thought processes to justify our F-bombing ways (mine anyway) and why we should play big.

From early on (think sixteen with a brand new license to run over curbs and knock over trash cans), I looked forward to my own set of wheels. If my parents had money (or if they were savvy *Go Big Ticket Now* F-bombers themselves), I may have gotten something halfway respectable to complement my level of swag. I was not so lucky, though. But I still longed for the day when I could get my own set of wheels. You know, that one car that turns heads faster than a two-year-old in church dropping his first F-bomb.

Now that I'm older, when I go shopping for a new car, the salesperson senses just how badly I want to drive away in the car of my choice. And get this; he's willing to work out a payment plan just for me. This is the exact opposite of what my parents or even my well-rounded "best" friends might lead me to believe. There is nothing like going to a car dealership and having someone on my side for a change.

These are good people. And to prove my point on this, go to a car dealership, eye something really flashy on the lot, and then sit down with the salesperson who comes out to shake your hand. Listen to him. What is one of the first things he asks? That's right, "What kind of monthly payments are you looking for?" And this is a favorite question among salespeople for just about any big ticket item you're looking at. It's like they all went to the same "satisfy the customer" school or something.

The beauty of the monthly payment approach is that it opens up a whole world of payment options. Some folks even run a zero-down option that makes it even more appealing, and of course, that much easier to get into the car of our dreams or whatever else we're looking to put our greedy little mitts on.

What's the catch, right? There is none. That's right, no catch. It's all in the fine print on those contracts we sign. And I've seen those contract payments get pretty darn low, like one-night-of-heavy-partying low. Just one night! Can you believe it?

Now to be fair to all those naysayers out there, it *will* take a little longer to pay off your purchase. But if it's a car, it will still hold some value, right? You simply sell it (or trade it back to the dealer) and get your next shiny, new car. And if you still owe a little bit on the car, I'm sure most dealers will be happy to roll that amount into your new loan. Heck, the dealer you bought your car from may even send you a letter in the mail, practically begging to buy your car back.

So go out and get the car of your dreams. Ride in style while it still matters, because once you settle down and have kids and dogs and cats and fish and hamsters and Lord only knows what else, that flashy new car may not fly over so well with your partner. But please don't forget that you can use this approach with boats, houses, timeshares, and anything else you have no business buying. You'll have a pretty good indication that you are about to F-bomb your finances when you hear those magic words: "What kind of monthly payments are you looking for?" Now get out there and *Go Big Ticket Now*!

Here's another *almost true* story by/about a real-life F-bomber to hammer it home.

This story is not from a family member of mine! Whew! It was beginning to seem like we had cornered the market on financial F-bombing, and that wouldn't be fair to the rest of the world. We'll call this guy Chet because it rhymes with 'debt.' Chet has a good job and believe it or not, he actually makes a lot of jack. Way more money than I've ever earned. He lives in a nice house. And you know that he drives a really nice car, because after all, this section is *Go Big Ticket Now*.

The thing about Chet is that he has a wife and kids and is still able to *Go Big Ticket Now*. Very impressive. The thing I love about Chet is that he seems to upgrade his house every three years or so. I know, right? It *is* nice.

Now picture a really fast sports car that gets maybe twelve MPG. You know, the kind of car you feel you should have to pay to look at. Well, Chet drives that car. And everyone knows it. Chet knows the value of looking good for clients. The funny thing is that even with all that jack, he can't afford all his stuff, especially because his wife is an F-bomber in denial.

The trouble with the *Go Big Ticket Now* approach, according to Chet, is that the banks you use to leverage those big ticket items can sometimes call your bluff. So Chet makes a lot of money, which allows him to borrow a lot more money, which throws a big F-bomb into his financial freedom. Chet cries a lot at night when no one else is looking. I can only imagine that these are tears of joy.

Lucky for Chet, he has a mom who will bail his butt out of trouble and give him even more money to spend. That is very cool because he is now turning his mom into a financial F-bomber too (I love it when families bond like this).

Do you now see how much control we F-bombers have in the world? It is quite staggering really. It almost makes you think that the military should save their "bombs" and instead hire us to go into warring countries and set up shop so that we could decimate from within, just like we do at home. And that should pay a lot of jack, my F-bombing friends!

Don't Research Before You Buy

This is definitely another favorite of mine because my background is scientific research. And to "just say no" (to research) is empowering. It slaps my trained perception in the face and forces the neurons in my brain to fire along a completely different path, getting them out of the ruts they've formed over the course of my entire life. Some people may think this could possibly lead to you peeing yourself, but I assure you, it would be something else entirely. . . like LOLROTF.

Don't Research Before You Buy allows me to act on impulse. How many times have you heard "Don't think, just do it?" All the greats have this trait. They block out all the voices in their heads, and bam, they just do it. Heck, advertising campaigns have been launched on this very notion. If these big corporations are spending millions of dollars to get the word out, then it must be really good stuff. So get out there and feed your impulsive ways. You'll wind up spending all your rent money on all sorts of crap you really don't need. And this could lead to possible eviction. Now that's financial F-bombing at its best.

Here's another *almost true* story by/about a real-life F-bomber to hammer it home.

Let's change my name to Ray because it rhymes with 'pay.' Ray is an educated, all-around smart dude (no really, I am). I married a smart dudette. I have a really smart kid. Do you get the picture here? We are too damn smart for our own good. Anyway, I took my lovely wife on a road trip to a fabulous vacation spot. We both loved it. The place had smart appliances, smart design, and we even used our smart phones to take pictures of all the smartness around us. And the best part is that we got the place for next to nothing, and without a lick of research. As a bonus, we got to go to the resort's main sales office for a tour of the property and an opportunity to get in on this place so that we could come back whenever we wanted.

So hand in hand, we went to the lovely presentation and toured the property. It was even nicer than we had first experienced. And to think, we could come back to this place (and others like it all over the world) for a small monthly payment (remember this sales tactic?). Sold. We did absolutely no research and walked right into this den, kicked up our feet, and called it home . . . all for a couple hundred bucks a month for the rest of our lives.

After the whole experience was over, we realized we had totally F-bombed our finances. How did we know? Research! It turns out that we paid ten times what we could have gotten this luxury deal for on eBay! I pulled off one of the most destructive F-bombs of all time, so good that when my son turns eighteen, I can choose to saddle him with this eternal debt as well. Out of everyone I know, I, of all people, take the cake for the best financial F-bombing.

So you see, F-bombing is an equal opportunity destroyer. You can be as smart as Ray (or as dumb as Ray), and still be an effective F-bomber. So say "No!" to research . . . at least until after those F-bombs have been released for action. After the fact, you can do whatever you want. F-bombers unite. I see an F-bomber Facebook page in the works. Can you see it too?

Buy Everything You Don't Need

This is such an old school way to F-bomb your finances, and boy am I good at it. When I go to the store, I look for items on sale and buy way more than I need. Toothpaste on sale? I buy three or four tubes. Any deodorants have those little "use it now" coupons taped to the package? I'll get a dozen (especially since I live in a warm climate). And when I shop this way, I actually get a sense of accomplishment because, deep down, I think I'm saving money. It's the old win-win scenario. And you can do this with everything!

Let's face it, a good old-fashioned sale will get most of us into a tizzy, and I'm no exception. I'll go into combat mode, searching the shelves with laser focus, edging other shopping carts out of the way (or intentionally angling my cart so that no one else even considers breaching my perimeter), and grabbing every color of something just in case I may need it later. Buying everything you don't need solves the issue of which ones to keep. Keep them all!

And it doesn't have to stop there. Do you like collecting things? Well, this is the section for you. I have a Wheaties box with my favorite athlete on it squirreled away in my attic. I'm holding on to that roach bait in hopes that those flakes will be frosted with gold after I sell the only one left in existence (unopened, by humans anyway) on eBay. Well, just think if I had been using this method to its fullest and bought ten boxes. That'd be ten times the profit! Ka-ching.

And you can collect anything. I've even seen a half ounce, 1950 miniature box of raisins listed on eBay for over half a million dollars. I'm serious! Can you imagine if that seller would have been following the *Buy Everything You Don't Need* technique? They would have bought a hundred of those things for like $2 if my math is as good as I know it is. One-hundred times half a million is 50,000,000 dollars. To put this into perspective, you could have F-bombed your finances back in 1950 (and that's including all the principles we've covered in this book), and you still would have wound up with $50,000,000 (assuming you got the sales) to retire on. And this is the reason F-bombing is such a popular sport among couch potatoes worldwide. It's almost as if all this stuff has been laid out ahead of time and no matter what we do, we will still end up with the same amount at the end of the day, which is what we were meant to have all along.

We even get to see inside the lives of collectors and people who buy everything they don't need on shows like *Hoarders*. Consider being immortalized on TV as a bonus. Isn't that everyone's dream? On these shows, they even talk about how people get to be hoarders and the psychological issues they must have. Of course you and I know that they just may be nothing more than old school F-bombers.

Perhaps after this book comes out and gets into the right hands, people will once and for all give F-bombers their due on shows like this. Then we can all root for them, pointing at the screen, saying, "Awesome use of *Buy Everything You Don't Need*! Bravo, my fellow F-bomber, bravo!" Tears follow.

Here's another *almost true* story by/about a real-life F-bomber to hammer it home.

We will call this girl Linda because it rhymes with 'spenda.' And before you ask, this is yet another relative story, but it is not about me, as I am too lazy and too weak to do this kind of heavy lifting. It is becoming evident, though, that this financial F-bombing stuff must be in my family's DNA (Do Not Achieve) make-up.

Linda is a collector. She has always been the ultimate collector of personal effects (sounds criminally serial, doesn't it). From an early age, she collected anything and everything to do with people. If I combed my hair for the first time, I knew Linda would not be far behind, grabbing the comb (and all the hair left behind) for her collection. The beauty of it was that as Linda collected items, she felt the need to purchase new items to collect. Classic, right?

Linda was a hoarder before there was even a word for it. She collected and she bought—everyday junk like Whoopee cushions, candy cigarettes, and novelty napkins. Stores started putting items close to the cash register because of her. And it was not that she necessarily bought in quantity, but that she bought and bought things she never needed.

This behavior went on for years, forcing her to have storage units in different states. And I think I may have even seen one of her units being auctioned off on an episode of *Storage Wars*. Oh, the memories! But there came a day when she no longer worked, as she had worn herself out with all that spending and hoarding, and she no longer had someone around to cover her expensive expenses.

She hit the proverbial rock-bottom. Have you ever seen rock-bottom, with all its jagged edges of despair? It's an F-bomber's paradise. And it's a really big place with plenty of rooms for all your friends and relatives. Well, Linda almost lost her life on those jagged edges thanks to her F-bombing ways. But she didn't, and that's the moral of the story. That which doesn't kill you, makes you stronger (or at least strong enough to F-bomb yourself another day).

Education

$e=mc^2$ →
$a+b^2=c^2$ →
$a>b>c$ →

→ $Ag+S$
→ $\xrightarrow{\Delta}$
→ $H_2 + U + Ge$

3

HOW TO F-BOMB YOUR EDUCATION

Intro

The sad truth is that most of us will have to earn a living by using our brains—as challenged as they may be. Less than 1% of us will be able to use our bodies to put food on the table. That one out of a hundred pretty much only includes porn stars and organ donors. And even though I think that on my best days that percentage could be a little higher, no one wants to see me in my underwear, let alone full Monty. And that organ donor gig is not as glitzy as it seems.

So as our educated brains are the only thing standing between us and urban urchin (think bum with attitude), education becomes more important than just about anything else we've got going. But still, there will be a few "I don't need no education" souls out there who wish to

F-bomb it all. For these folks, I have come up with a few bona fide ways to hose your education. They will not totally destroy it, but they can lead to enough damage to keep you in a dead end job (but off the streets, because quite frankly, it is just hard for me to look at that).

Go It Alone

This tactic speaks to our sense of "If you want something done right, then do it yourself!" I can't tell you how many times I heard that growing up (usually muttered under my father's breath). Of course as an enterprising young man with too much time on my hands and no social life, I learned to purposefully botch things up to get out of doing those things I felt were beneath me, which happened to be just about everything outside of praying to be removed as the perennial poster child for bad skin.

Going it alone can have that loner, tough guy appeal, but when tied to education, it makes you a rebel without applause. There aren't many people out there (even that weirdo who's been stalking you for the last few months) who will give you props for F-bombing your education. It's just not a cool thing to do. For instance, no one really *wants* me to be stupid. Sure they want to call me stupid and be way smarter than I'll ever be, but they really don't want me to be "about as sharp as a marble." It must have something to do with survival of the species or something else equally challenging.

So how do you *Go It Alone*? Well, for one, you just go it alone, i.e. you do it yourself without any help from others. Some people see asking for help as a weakness, and since only the strong survive, it seems to make perfect sense.

With my being overly stubborn and always right, it took me a while to figure out that "Only the strong survive" is actually a true statement, but that my definition of strong was a little weak. Strong to me was standing tall in the face of danger, having sleek, bulging muscles, and being unyielding like my grandmother refusing to give me her secret mac-n-cheese recipe. But standing tall only got my ass kicked, working out got me muscle cramps, and being unyielding got me to total jerk status (but the kind of jerk who doesn't get the girl). In a word, I was weak.

After years of muscle cramps and "go to hell" looks, I understood that strength has more to do with that lump of matter in between my ears than anything else. Our brains have two sides to them, just like most of the stories I tell. Some brain matter gathers education and stores it like an SD card, while other brain matter tells us what to do. Most F-bombers don't like being told what to do, so hosing your education is not too difficult. Just think what happens when your brain doesn't exactly know what to do. It expects us to ask for help and exhibit that strong behavior so that maybe we can make it out of that burning building alive.

Our brains see asking for help as the ultimate sign of strength, so it stands to reason that *Going It Alone* will take you back to the days of my old school stubborn reality, where strength was using my 8" guns to impress the ladies and my 12" thighs to run away when it didn't work.

Going it alone also includes shutting down the ear holes. Just don't listen. It's an oldie but goodie for sure. When I listen, I have to pay attention. And when I pay attention, I learn stuff. So if you ever feel yourself falling prey to listening, just repeat these words to the speaker, "You are stupider than me, so leave me alone!" It'll be tough because that mind of yours thinks it's programmed to achieve. Just hang in there. The whole world is against you on this one, so stay old school strong!

Here's another *almost true* story by/about a real-life F-bomber to hammer it home.

Let's change my name to Rufus because it rhymes with 'doofus.' Rufus is a smart guy (as I've already stated), even though you probably thought he would be stupid given that we are F-bombing education in this chapter. One day, I went to the gym with a buddy to work out and meet girls. Well on this particular day, I saw a stunning beauty on the lat machine. I, being very familiar with lats, decided to "work in" and strike up a conversation.

My buddy offered to coach me, but I wouldn't have it; I had this after all. And the conversation went much better than I could have ever expected—so good that I considered asking this girl to an upcoming event that my parents were having. My buddy casually listened while working out on the machine next to us. Again he tried to intervene but I had this, so again, I brushed him off. It looked like this girl would actually go with me to the event, so I obviously made it sound much less boring than it inevitably would be, and I of course said nothing about it being my parents' party. Eventually, the stunning beauty and I parted ways. And then, and only then, did I meet back up with my buddy.

Wearing a big smile on my face, I said, "She said she usually works out around ten in the morning, so it's lucky that we even met at all. I wonder what she does that allows her to work out during the middle of the day . . ."

My buddy looked at me. "Dude, she's a stripper!"

"Oh, yeah, I guess that would explain it," I said, recalling other things she had said, like "my professional name is Jade."

"I tried to tell you but—"

"How in the hell would you know?"

"I listen bro," he laughed. "And you're the smart one?"

Now I told this story to get your mind wrapped around various forms of education.

Make no mistake, education is everywhere. Yes, it is school, but it is also life. Even if you're Joe Cool or Smarty Arty, you can still be Rufus Doofus. But don't listen to me, just *Go It Alone* and see for yourself. Socrates said that a wise man is he who knows he knows nothing. So insist that you got it and stay stupid, my friend.

Sleep In

I work and play hard, so why not get in the habit of sleeping in? That's what I used to think. And as sleeping in does wonders for your complexion, this was always high on my list as an acne-plagued teenager. Heck, getting some sleep never sounded so good. But my complexion never cleared up and I started missing too much play time.

"Sleeping in" is the wicked stepsister to "the early bird gets the worm." Just to be clear, I don't really believe that old adage. I've seen plenty of fat birds that don't even look like they can roll out of the nest in the morning, much less swoop down and fight off all those scrappy, early risers for that lone worm. But I do believe in the metaphor or lesson that the early bird attempts to teach us (remember I'm no longer a true F-bomber in the education sense).

The essence, as I see it, is to simply show up. How could such a life lesson be so unassuming? It's based on what I alluded to in the last section—it's inherent in our ancestral chemistry that we advance through learning. So a lot of times, just showing up is half the battle. Sleep in and you become a no-show, a lost cause, an F-bomber.

Sleeping in is so easy to do, and it's even a natural response, especially after having too much fun the night before. This is another one of those ironies. We're programmed to learn, yet our bodies tell us to get our rest. I won't bring the soul into this right now, but let me tell you, the mind and body have been fighting since the two of them got together.

To our brains and bodies, sleeping in is like that argument between my parents that keeps replaying every Thanksgiving. Not only does it divide two seemingly inseparable entities, but it's downright embarrassing, especially when I have my fake friends over. And to think that our bodies and our minds bicker about this crap constantly! It's like they're fighting for control over us. And given our F-bombing ways, this is comedy in its truest form. If you don't see that, no worries. Maybe you should just go sleep on it.

Here's another *almost true* story by/about a real-life F-bomber to hammer it home.

We will call him Ronin because it rhymes with 'serotonin.' Ronin liked to drink in college. Ronin liked to party in college. Ronin liked to drink and party in college (that rules me out, as

I was not that cool in college). See where this is going? I'm cutting this one short because I need a nap.

Ronin slept in a lot. Professors noted Ronin never went to class. Ronin scheduled those ten o'clock classes, so Ronin is to blame. You may have had some of those eight o'clock slots, but then you probably had no desire to F-bomb your education either. You are only reading this because you are an over-achiever and read books from cover to cover. But this is about Ronin. Yes, he is a nobody, but this is still his story. So let's get back to it. Yawn.

Ronin slept in. Ronin failed classes. Ronin slept in and failed classes. Want to fail classes and F-bomb your education? Sleep in and never go to class. I don't know whatever happened to Ronin, but I'm fairly certain that he's still sleeping in? How could I dare speculate? Because years of killing brain cells destroys the brain's will to fight. And to think, he could have been a contender . . .

Do It Tomorrow

This gives the procrastinator carte blanche to F-bomb their education. I've been known to procrastinate with the best of them. "I'll do it tomorrow!" was my old battle cry, another tired saying used when I was too tired or too busy to care. In the end, things that get put off until tomorrow are not worth doing today. And to someone F-bombing their education, is anything really worth doing today? When I put something off, what am I telling the world? What am I telling myself?

I'm curious. Can you go back in time? No? I don't have 1.21 gigawatts lying around either. One more question: can you go into the future? Same answer applies doesn't it? To rational beings, this would indicate that we only have the present moment we're in (E.g. I happen to be writing, and you happen to be reading). That's all we ever have, isn't it? So technically, we don't have tomorrow.

For me, if I choose not to do something in the moment (like buy *another* five boxes of Girl Scout cookies), I'm telling the world that it's not something of importance to me, at least when I say it anyway. So when I say I'll do it tomorrow, it's my way of saying, "Piss off because I'm not interested." And when the brain is conditioned to do it tomorrow, that tomorrow hardly ever comes.

Doing it tomorrow also forces me to stay in the same place and never learn anything or get anywhere because I actually never do anything. It is like quicksand. Fight it if you must, but you'll only sink a little deeper. Before long, it becomes hard to breathe, and then bits of you start to die off. It's quite ghastly, and it is so hard to pull off "pale," especially when you don't have those vampiric good looks. So I must leave this one to those bloodsuckers willing to suck the life right out of their education.

Here's another *almost true* story by/about a real-life F-bomber to hammer it home.

We will call him Roger because it rhymes with 'dodger.' Ol' Roger. God love 'em. When someone says that, it usually means that another someone is a major F-bomber. I'm sure "God love 'em" has been said a lot about Roger. I don't particularly care for Roger. Why? Because being around him gets old (it used to be like looking in a mirror, and I'm not that attractive).

You see, Roger is a dreamer. He is going to do so many things that I really don't think there is enough time in the world to accomplish them. Still, Roger throws them out there like candy at Halloween, his words ghostly apparitions waiting to one day materialize and signal the end of days.

With Roger, the answer to everything is tomorrow. But then tomorrow comes and nothing happens. This is where I learned all about there being no tomorrow. And Apollo Creed confirmed this for me in *Rocky III*.

But what about today? Roger doesn't like today. Today is for planning. Tomorrow is where all the action takes place. Don't believe me? Just ask Roger. He'll tell you. By the way, Roger still hasn't amounted to much, and neither will you if you do it tomorrow. So put it all off and never get a damn thing done. History teaches us this. Don't believe me? Go look it up. Or better yet, just *Do It Tomorrow*.

Get a Hobby

I can hear the sighs from those who know me well. This was one of mine from way back. No, keep going back a little further. Yeah, it's that far back. I have been named king of the Hobby Shelf. I have bookcases dedicated to hobbies, none being too boring for me. Sewing, perfumery, weightlifting, tennis, martial arts, candle making, aromatherapy, travel, and you know that list keeps on going.

It was out from beneath the hobby shelf that I had to rise and shake off the F-bombing dust (some of those books were pretty old). And it makes me that much more knowledgeable to discuss it. Only if you're a recovering get-a-hobby addict can you fully comprehend the power of this method and truly understand how it can obliterate your education. So listen up potential F-bombers; you are about to be schooled by the master.

Why do people say, "Go get a hobby?" Well, for me, it was because they didn't want me in their face. But it was also because they thought I needed something to do so that I wouldn't come off so creepy. Could this be another move to protect mankind? Perhaps they were saying that I needed to learn something, to broaden my horizon so I wouldn't dumb down the species. But the problem is that their innocent advice could have kept me from my greater purpose. Yes, it's more of that irony stuff.

You see, a good hobby does a great job of *diverting* our attention. It keeps us focused on something that is probably meaningless in the grand scheme. And this in turn does little for the species. Education, and more importantly, learning, is the world's greatest weapon against otherworldly problems. So when the aliens come to take over all our stuff, they will be looking to attack all those who have F-bombed their education, i.e. the weak links. And this is one of those things that is bad for business.

If the aliens get you, you will have little need to F-bomb other areas of your life because you will be alien hors d'oeuvres. But what if when they ate you, some of your F-bomb DNA got intertwined with theirs? Maybe there would be a whole new market for training F-bombers. Still, it's just not worth it for me. I would probably have to learn a new language and wear some kind of Merlin hat. I'm not into role playing, and I look terrible in hats! So don't *Get a Hobby*. You will just end up being eaten by aliens, and I will look utterly ridiculous. Please refer to one of the other sections to F-bomb your education. This one is starting to freak me out.

Here's another *almost true* story by/about a

real-life F-bomber to hammer it home.

Let's change my name to King Fuzi because it rhymes with 'doozy.' There once was a dork named Fuzi, who one day fell and got woozy. This dork looked around, and all that was found, was a hobby they all called Floozy.

I would go on but this is a PG-rated show. As you can imagine, Floozy did a great job of diverting my attention. This kept me from learning all the stuff that I was supposed to learn in college. After graduation, to pay homage to Floozy, I spent years engulfed in every hobby imaginable. I learned how to F-bomb education with authority and now secretly watch and wait for an alien invasion.

4

HOW TO F-BOMB YOUR SOCIAL LIFE

Intro

Having a social life shows our ability to mix and mingle and be one with all the other miscreants in the world. It is how we attract our clan or tribe (not to be confused with family, as they're sort of stuck with us). Our social life is important because it too is integral to the continuation of the species.

But to an F-bomber, having *no* social life can be beneficial in a myriad of ways. For instance, it gives us the opportunity to hang out with our cats. It gives us time to get really good at arts and crafts. And it gives us all the time we'll ever need to come up with those perfect comeback one-liners that we could have used when society was dissing us like old school plague. So let the following methods be your friends, because they'll lead to the only friends you'll ever have.

Cover Your Spread

Okay, you probably have a few things in mind here. Let me assure you, they are both wrong. *Cover Your Spread* simply relates to our social eating habits, and make no mistake, these habits can decimate our social life. Now let's dig in (an unintentional food reference that tells me I really must be onto something).

One of the best ways to cover your spread (think spread of food if you still haven't gotten it yet) is to simply sneeze on the party platter. That's right; blow that spew out of your mouth at an impressive 35 mph and up to 20 feet! Trust me, I've seen this in slo-mo, and it is truly amazing. We can launch mucus from across the room, so we don't even need to be directly over the party platter. And if you think that thin sheet of Plexiglas over the buffet is going to keep anything out, think again. The physics of spit spray dictates that angles are involved, and when those angles get going, the blast radius becomes deadly.

Being the guy who chronically blows on everyone's food will end your social life before it begins. I've personally stopped to look at all the sour faces in the room after I ah-ah-ahchooh. None of those people want to be my friend by the way.

Another avenue to *Cover Your Spread* is the old classic—double dipping. First I'll get the stare-down and then a stern warning. But those chips don't taste as good without the salsa, so I'll still try to slip in the old double dip where it doesn't belong. *No one will notice,* I think. But everyone notices, and they even keep score! And guess who's never on the invite list again? That would be the person who brought my sorry ass to the party, because as a master of this technique, I would not have been invited in the first place. So now I have F-bombed the potential social life I might have had with those at the party, and I really F-bombed the only social life I've got.

You can get really imaginative on different ways to cover your spread, but in the interest of time, I will provide you with only one more gem. If you're a guy, or you've ever been to a bar or club with unisex bathrooms, you've no doubt noticed something strangely peculiar. And that is that some men tend to faux wash their hands. You've seen them (hell you may be one of them). They saunter up to the sink, look in the mirror, turn on the water, wiggle the tips of their fingers in the water, turn the water off, and then rub their hands through their hair or on their shirts before getting back to the party.

Why would anyone fake wash their hands? Because someone else is watching! Otherwise they wouldn't have even stopped at the sink. Are you fooling anyone, Dirty Hand Bandit?

People take note of this and tell their friends so that they can eke out disgusting sounds every time you dig into the chip bowl.

Now not only has Dirty Hand Bandit spread his mutant germs everywhere, but he's also F-bombed his social life. If you question whether the technique is working, just tell everyone that you never wash your hands. Don't want to do that? Well, that shame and guilt should tell you that it's F-bombing at its best. But then if you carry that shame, I'd have to question whether or not your heart is really in it. If not, then lather up because F-bombing your social life is probably not for you.

Here's another *almost true* story by/about a real-life F-bomber to hammer it home.

We will call him Nick because it rhymes with 'sick.' Nick's a pretty cool guy (so you know this is not me) in a lot of respects. He's a pretty good chess player too. And being such, he has great hands. But he likes to put those hands in all sorts of places. Up his nose, in his ears, down his drawers, and everywhere else.

Being a chesslete, Nick has a healthy appetite for vegetables (he's a vegan), but strangely, no one else has an appetite when he's ready to dig in. Nick eats alone in the cafeteria. The problem is that Nick never notices that people have their eyes on him, and it's not because he's mouth-watering eye candy. Plain and simple, he's a digger. And all that digging eventually leads to covering the spread.

Nick is a cool name. It's one of those names you could be friends with. But Nick doesn't have a lot of friends. Nick plays chess and he always covers the spread. Nick is an F-bomber.

Now I know what you're thinking, but Nick *really* is a cool vegan chesslete. He's the only one I know, so that goes a long way in my book. But given everything that is great about Nick, people can't get past him covering the spread. So go dig yourself (almost the title of this section but too limiting) and *Cover Your Spread*!

Blend In

This is awesome for F-bombing your social life or for being a secret assassin. If you are a secret assassin, then your social life is probably already F-bombed, and I issue you one of the few passes I give to readers in this book. This pass allows you to blend yourself right on into the next chapter. If you decide to keep reading, though, try not to blend into the words because it may freak you out if you see yourself. I take no responsibility for blowing anyone's cover or the results that may arise from self introspecttion. And yes, I realize that last phrase was redundant, but I did it to flesh out that blending-in guy.

Blending in is just that. We become all that is

around us. Think "uninteresting," and therefore, drawing no attention to oneself (something I'm extremely good at). Have you ever gone to a party and noticed the people that cling to the walls like last year's old paint? Yes? Well then say hello to me because the only people who see me are other blenders. We blend in, remember?

People with awesome social lives don't clutter their aesthetic with drab and boring, unless it is for some wild, zany party that someone dreamed up to actually be drab and boring. But then they would still have great social lives because their creativity in trying to be drab and boring would be hilarious. For these people, F-bombing their social life is just not going to happen no matter how hard they try. So if you are one of these people, move along; there is nothing to see here.

Blending in is not just about looking invisible, it's about being invisible on the inside too. Even *I* get thrown a bone every now and then, and when I do, I still somehow maintain my F-bombed social status. How do I do it? Well, I get so excited over being noticed that I start to mirror whoever it is that sees me (that's the sincerest form of flattery by the way). Essentially, I do what they do.

If someone takes a particular viewpoint, I take the same one. I blend into their way of thinking. As it turns out, when I do this well enough, I am seen as a parrot, repeating everything someone else says and thus giving the illusion that I can't think for myself (which is total crap because I do dress myself every day). Either that, or I am seen as a mockingbird, an insulting and incredulous SOB. I'm usually so F-bombed that no one ever invites me to do anything ever again! I've learned that this technique really douses the flames to keep them burning strong. Before long, my social life is once again just a pile of ashes. Now go get 'em tigers! (or should that be chameleons?)

Here's another *almost true* story by/about a real-life F-bomber to hammer it home.

We will call her Annalee because it rhymes with 'can't see.' Annalee is a girl I knew in high school. Wait, where'd she go. I only know that I went to school with Annalee because she told me so years later at a reunion. She was even in some of my classes, and . . . what was I talking about again. Man, this girl's good. It's like I'm in a crazy amnesic trance. Anyway, Annalee was telling me at this reunion . . . wait, is someone at the door? Where was I? Oh yeah. This Annalee girl was . . . oh what's the point! I still can't remember a damn thing, and I'm starting to wonder if that reunion encounter was last night's dream. In short, blend in to F-bomb your social life and drive people insane in the future when they try to remember who in the heck you were!

Tell It Like It Is

"Tell it like it is" is something else I hear all the time. I think you'll agree in a few moments that this further proves that society is geared to F-bomb itself. I hope that some of you are already doing this technique, and that as a result, your social lives are in the proverbial toilet along with mine. I of course only want this to further validate the technique.

Nothing has F-bombed my social life in years past like being a rat, a.k.a. the snitch. This is supreme telling it like it is because it goes after another person, and it always makes me feel like a heroic vigilante of truth. For example, if someone just let a stinker get through their gabardine, I would deflect and point to the real culprit. Not only does this clear my good name, but it also does the group a solid by letting everyone know to stay away from Old Rumbles. Telling it like it is keeps you in the clear, but it also pisses everyone else off in the process. Take that, social life!

One more form of *Tell It Like It Is* is talking about yourself. And why not? I have a lot to say. So whenever I actually get an ear or two, I bend those babies until they break. Nothing attracts people to you like always talking about yourself. If you're astute, you may be thinking that this might actually repel people. And I cannot lie, it's like fart spray to a florist.

Here's another *almost true* story by/about a real-life F-bomber to hammer it home.

We will call her Karen because it rhymes with 'sharin'.' Karen is one of those women who seemingly has it all together. She is smart. She is married. She has loving kids. She lives in a mansion. She kicks ass at work. And she has pretty cool neighbors. But alas, she is one helluva F-bomber in the social landscape.

Why? Well given the title of this section, you should know that she tells it like it is. But in which form does her rambling take shape? Drum roll please. Okay that was corny, but so is . . . talking about yourself with every dying breath (believe me, I know). And is she the queen! Karen is the best in the business. No matter how good I think I am, Karen is way better. I have personally seen her turn the conversation back around to herself when someone was talking about tree fungus (that was one wild party).

So while Karen thinks that all her talking and sharing is productive in building up her social life, she only manages to build a house of cards (all face cards with her picture on them of course). The irony is that every time she opens her mouth, that house comes tumbling down. I like irony. I like Karen. Karen is an awesome F-bomber. Karen doesn't know that she is an F-bomber. Or then again, maybe she does know. She is very smart. Maybe she doesn't want the hassle of a social life. Maybe she wrote the proverbial book on this technique. I think I like Karen even more now! But not in a social way, which of course would make her happy. Well played, Karen. Well played indeed!

Look Out for Numero Uno

Looking out for yourself is just common sense, which makes this method second nature. We all do it. If I'm walking down the street and a big sinkhole suddenly appears, do you think I keep walking and wait for someone to tell me what to do? Heck no. I take action. This is looking out for numero uno. There won't always be someone around to yell at me (even though it seems inevitable at times), so I've learned to sharpen this skill over time to survive.

Looking out for numero uno in the "group" setting is, strangely, not well-accepted. Somewhere along the way, it has become associated with selfishness when done in the presence of others. Take away all those people, and it's okay. And if we did anything other, all those people would call us idiots. This is more of that irony that I love so much.

But don't think that this only applies to life-or-death situations because it is so much bigger than that. It could be innocent like taking three bags of chips to a party and then taking home what's not eaten. I know it seems fine to do this on the surface, but for me it led to party people calling me an *acquaintance*—nothing more than party fodder—filling the room to make everyone else that much more interesting by comparison.

Looking out for numero uno could even be diving in to take the last hors d'oeuvre. There is a reason no one ever eats the last one. As an F-bomber, you *want* to be labeled as that guy. Other ways of looking out for numero uno are opening the door for only you, taking the best seat, getting only yourself a drink, and shaking your booty to only the songs you like. I understand these things may seem like little things, but trust me, they all seek and destroy your social life.

But perhaps the best aspect of looking out for numero uno is being a taker, as in taking more than you give back. When you do this crap, you're F-bombing dreams will be a reality. As I could write another book on this topic alone, I will give up only one example (how's that for a taker attitude?). See how innocent it looks?

Let's say I go out to a club and get some pretty good service, even though my bartender has had people hitting her with lewd comments all night. What should I do?

A) Tell her to hang in there because it'll get better
B) Ask her what took her so long to get my drink
C) Ask her if she wants to hook up later
D) Give her a good 15% tip for her efforts

E) Give her 20+% and think it should be more

As an F-bomber in training, I sure hope you said anything but E, because those answers could label me as a taker. I took good service, but I did not give back proportionately. When people in your social group see this, you become known as the turd, and while some turds float, most sink right to the bottom. I've learned that being labeled a turd is much worse than being labeled a dork. I guess turds are just gross, and social lives don't like gross.

Here's another *almost true* story by/about a real-life F-bomber to hammer it home.

We will call her Ruth because it rhymes with 'uncouth.' Ruth was new to the group. The group went out for girls' night (evidence that this is not me, not because I'm not a girl but because multiple girls were involved). The girls ate shrimp, had drinks and more drinks, and talked for hours. Ruth fit in nicely. She could eat. She could drink. And she could talk. Ruth was happy. The girls were happy to have another person join their group.

Then came the bill. All the girls reached for the bill except for one. Yes, it was Ruth. But in Ruth's defense, she wasn't there. You see, Ruth went to the bathroom when the check finally came. And the fact that Ruth was not there to reach for the check was of course no problem with the group. They all knew that bladders were like husbands—ignore them too long, and you might be fighting an infection later.

What the girls *did* have issue with was what happened next. They told Ruth that they decided to split the bill equally among them to make it easy. "But wait," Ruth insisted. She was drinking the cheap box wine, while some of the other girls were going after the pricey stuff. This hardly seemed fair. Ruth said that she would gladly pay for what she consumed. And at the end of the day, that's exactly what she did. She courageously spoke up, looking out for numero uno.

But wait, the story does not end there. The other girls were forced to do math, and this usually does not make a group of loaded women very happy. "Who invited her anyway," seeped from under someone's breath. "This is utterly ridiculous," fell from another. And before long, the old "This is the last time we ever do this!" echoed through the air.

And just like that, Ruth's social life was F-bombed beyond repair. To the other girls, Ruth sat there all night taking their time, hospitality, and witty conversation only to give back what she drank. The only thing she could have done better to F-bomb her social outing would've been to eat the last grilled shrimp that lay alone on that otherwise devoured platter. All in all, a good effort though. This goes to show you that it is never too late in the evening to F-bomb your social life.

PART 2: THE OTHER YEARS

Marriage

5

HOW TO F-BOMB YOUR MARRIAGE

Intro

I realize two things. One: you may have yet to put a ring on it. And two: I will get a month's worth of dirty looks for writing this chapter. But in the event you ever do make it to the big show (and I have mysteriously dis-appeared), I want you to have the tools to F-bomb that blissful union whenever you see fit. And for the rest of you who've already joined the club, see how many of these F-bomb tactics you already employ. It is of course best to implement as many of these strategies as you can to be the most successful.

And don't be scared to mix it up. Being one-dimensional is boring and predictable, and thus expected. This is also very dangerous to the F-bomber in the marriage arena, as spouses will start making excuses for you. E.g. "He always does that!" or "That's just the way she is!" I hate it when a good F-bombing effort is cheapened like this. You've put in a lot of hours F-bombing your life, and the last thing you need is someone not respecting all that hard work.

Lucky for you, I've got some insider intel on F-bombing your marriage. There are two people in my family with nine marriages between them. You think they don't know a thing or two about hosing a marriage? And I'm not talking about the obvious things like shagging your partner's sister or locking your in-laws in the basement.

I will caution you here. F-bombing your marriage does not necessarily end in divorce. Many times it will over time, but divorce is not a guaranteed result, because unbeknownst to you, chances are you picked someone with a lot of your same qualities. Some of these qualities may not be apparent now but are nonetheless still present on some level.

Now before you say that your partner is nothing like you, consider this: it's not so much that if you're an angry person, then your partner will be an angry person. But it is rather that if you're an angry person, then your partner may be well-conditioned to deal with that anger as if it were a normal aspect of life. And it would even go so far as your partner becoming the angry person if you suddenly lost all of your anger; it's as if anger were a necessary component of the union between you two. I've seen this in my own marriage, so I've got cred. It's very confusing, I know, but it's very real. So in short (or too long at this point), just remember that divorce is not a guarantee, but the methods in this chapter will go a long way in making you or your partner wish you were divorced, which is essentially just as good.

Always Be Right

I'm sure you've met people like this. If you've met me, then you definitely have. No matter the topic, we act as if we're renowned subject matter experts. We are annoying individuals. And if you're thinking that we're annoying beyond belief, then pat yourself on the back because you are probably one of us. Remember when you told all of your little schoolyard hoodlums that it takes one to know one? Well that logic still applies here in the big boy world. So return to your youth and get back to knowing everything.

Now you may be saying "that's not me," and if you are, this could be denial. While denial is also a highly effective F-bomb technique, it is out of place in this arena. So own up to yourself and be an adult. And if you truly are not the *Always Be Right* person, then maybe you should practice this method because it can be such an irritation to your partner.

Being right is easy. Start small if you have to. $2 + 2 = 4$. My dad can beat up your dad. Then once you get comfortable with it, take it to the next level. E.g. Me: "The sky is blue." Not Me: "No, it's cloudy." Me: "First of all, cloudy is not a color currently recognized by the scientific community as being the result of absorbed or scattered light. And secondly, the sky is still blue above those stratus clouds (to be more precise)." See how this method can be especially irritating? But be careful, my wife wants to kick my teeth in when I do this. (And this is the real reason I wear both a night guard and a cup to bed each night).

To always be right may seem like a heavy burden, but it doesn't have to be. Just use your words with conviction. Say them so smoothly that, by comparison, a baby's butt would feel like the skin of that 98 year-old sun goddess who hangs out at the pool all day. And please don't confuse this with lying. Everyone knows that if you truly believe something, then it is not a lie. So, believe in yourself for Pete's sake!

So why does this method work so well in the marriage arena? Marriage is built upon accepting imperfections and agreeing to put up with that BS until the end of time. It's implicit in the contract that we cooperate and bend when necessary. Always being right does not allow for that flexibility; it is instead, rigid and unyielding. Result: Yogi you are not, but Yoda, you are!

Here's another *almost true* story by/about a

real-life F-bomber to hammer it home.

We will call this girl Chloe because it rhymes with 'knowy.' Chloe is a sweet girl, college-educated, and not too bad to look at. She met Mr. Chloe one day and thought he was the cat's meow. I may have dressed a decade behind, but my body had obviously been chiseled by the gods themselves (didn't see that one coming, did you?). This enchanted Chloe, so much that she started doodling Mr. Chloe on her files at work just to see what it looked like on paper. We talked for hours on the phone each day and conversation never got boring. So Chloe thought it was time to date and make it official.

Lucky for her, Halloween was right around the corner. She decided to throw a grand party to make the announcement. She invited hundreds of her friends along with my two friends. We then went shopping for costumes together. I had equal say at this time in the relationship, while Chloe held her tongue for fear that it just may etch that beautiful marble that Mr. Chloe (yep, it's still me dreaming) was crafted from. Things progressed at a frenetic pace and soon we were married. The contract was signed and it was official.

Then things started to change. All of a sudden, Chloe not only had an opinion about everything but let me know about it. And it soon became apparent to me that Chloe was one of those people who always had to be right, and it irritated me beyond belief because I was the always-had-to-be-right person.

She carried on like this for a while until she happened to take a business course that forced her to look deep inside herself. Chloe's heart was ripped, and her highly successful practice of always being right ended right there and then. I later admitted to Chloe that before she went to the training class, I was ready to throw in the towel (into the laundry basket that is, as I knew that Chloe was still the best thing I had going). Chloe and I are still together. I even went through the training myself, but unfortunately for all those around me, it did little to cure my need to always be right.

Even though the ultimate F-bomb was averted in this story, I hope it highlights just how good *Always Be Right* is. If it had not been for that business training, things would have surely ended up differently. Chloe could have been the next president, and I would have become the First Lady Man (how embarrassing for an always-be-righter).

Never Argue

I know you may think that arguing is the *perfect* way to F-bomb your marriage, especially if you are still single. And on the surface, it seems transparent. But it's really as cloudy as drug testing for today's professional athletes.

"But wait," you may say, "my parents argued

all the time and they're now divorced." I don't doubt this, but I could give you more examples of couples who argue all the time and are *still* married. It's my guess that your parents got divorced because of something else, i.e. the arguing was only a byproduct. I hate to tell you this, Sport, but they could have gotten a divorce because of you. This is harsh and wrong for me to say on so many levels without context, but it could still be reality. Maybe you should've moved out before you turned thirty . . .

So why do people argue? See if you can pick the right answer as to why people argue.

 A) They disagree about something
 B) They don't like the other person
 C) They always have to be right
 D) They like hearing themselves talk
 E) They are hoping for a make-up shag
 F) A and B
 G) A and C
 H) A and D
 I) A and E
 J) All of the above

I hope you at least included A in your guess, as I had it in 60% of the answers. Actually, they're all right, aren't they? We could argue this, but that is exactly what I'm trying to get you to avoid doing (unless it is supporting your efforts to obnoxiously always be right). The problem with arguing is that there is often times something called conflict resolution, negotiation, and happy endings. Does that sound like F-bombing to you?

Arguing has the nasty tendency of fleshing out into reality those annoying little things we all do. And once those babies are on the table, some well-intentioned F-bombers will pick them up and start playing with them like they were puzzle pieces to life's mystery. This is dangerous! Put the apple down and step away from the tree. The next thing you know, you two lovebirds will be apologizing and saying things like "no, I'm sorry, Sweetie" and "not as sorry as I am, Snookums." And then your marriage has installed this F-bomb shield around it, making it that much harder to tear it all down. Please don't do this. It is not a pretty sight for any of us innocent bystanders caught in the crossfire.

Another thing about arguing is that it can put both people on equal footing in the marriage. Arguments have a back and forth nature, without which, you would have more of a lecture. We may start the marriage on equal footing, but to truly F-bomb that sucker, it goes a long way to make a shift where there is a great imbalance. When we don't argue anymore, it symbolizes that someone has given up, or that they don't care, or even that they're afraid. All great for F-bombers! So get involved in all the lectures you want, but stay away from those arguments.

HOW TO F-BOMB YOUR MARRIAGE

Here's another *almost true* story by/about a real-life F-bomber to hammer it home.

We will call her Max (short for Maxine which rhymes with 'damn mean') because it rhymes with 'lax.' Once upon a time, in a land right down the street from you, there lived a funny little lady named Max. Max was a passionate lass with interests far and wide. She loved to cook, she loved to sew, and tomatoes she loved to grow. It was not long before this lass found a lad, and each other for eternity they soon had.

Marriage was heaven and bliss, each day starting with a kiss. This couple was cute, so said the town, but on one day, Max became mute. She would not argue, she would not cuss, and older men cried, "So what's all the fuss!" The young lad knew something was wrong, it was as if he didn't belong.

And marriage became hell without bliss, each day starting with only a hiss. Max showed expression with another girl, with such delight her dress did twirl. But not around the lad, nevermore, no way, and it became quite sad, this scene each day. Around everyone else he felt quite tall, but around his wife, he was nothing but small. No emotion, no life came from her soul, but at least it was time for the Super Bowl.

So the lad watched the game with all of his friends, caring not who would lose or who would win. They all ate and cheered and were quite merry, but after the game, a world of hurt he did carry. Max started to speak but with reprimand, and this the lad could not stand. The lad was told that he was no good, his family not right 'cause they lived in the hood. The lad never argued but took this as fact, but his ego for now was seemingly cracked. Max and the lad went on for a while but it seemed more like a Swedish mile. Then they decided to end the ruse, F-bombing the marriage with a really short fuse.

You might think that Max and the lad were doomed because they did everything in rhymes and riddles, but it was because they never really argued. They never got all those pieces out on the table to see if a pretty picture would emerge. Instead, they were victims of each other. Both eventually never arguing, and thus, double F-bombing their fates. But you're right, that rhyming BS would get old pretty quick.

Refuse to Listen

Remember in the previous section how I said that those arguing parents probably got divorced for something deeper than a little surface squabbling? Well, I think it was refusing to listen that was at the core of that rotten apple. So listen up (or don't actually) because this could be that diamond in the rough that leads to the ultimate marriage F-bomb.

Have you ever given someone the stop sign

when they were in mid-speech? I have. It's like my inner crossing guard comes out and I've got my palm in their face to prove it. I'm telling them that I don't want to hear it. Little kids do this by plugging their ears with their fingers, which I think is truly a better option if you don't want to listen. But whichever way you choose to express it, *Refuse to Listen.*

When I listen to someone, I show them a degree of respect, as I am sitting there wasting my precious time doing it. It may be that I'm just waiting for my turn to speak, but what if I have locked horns with a rambler? I'll be in for a long ride with no out-of-state plates to count. And if you're like me, you're not going to get up and leave when this happens because you've already got too much invested at this point. Now it becomes a personal challenge to see if you can endure and show what you're made of. I'm sorry, but that blows all the way around.

The beauty is that refusing to listen is so easy to do, and you're probably doing it right now in your marriage. I just want you to realize it so that you can ratchet it up a notch for more F-bombing potential. Think about how many times you've been watching your show, and your partner interrupts with a question or comment. Your head may nod and you may even give some subconscious verbal response, but in reality, you have no idea what was said. And then your partner starts making statements like, "You don't love me anymore."

So find anything in the house to distract you. For the fellas, TV, music, and magazines with lots of pictures work best. For the ladies, all you need is a smartphone. This will lead to: "He cares more about his football games than our children!" or "She cares more about that damn phone than me!" When these types of statements fill the air, they weigh it down like sumo gas. And don't worry about that reference to the kids; she is actually referring to herself but is too embarrassed and hurt to admit it. Not to mention that the sumo gas took out the children long ago.

So to review, listening shows respect, shows you care, shows your interest, and can take a really long time if your day is a real suckfest. So plug your ears, hold up your hand, fake a sneezing attack, or even walk away. Just *Refuse to Listen*.

Here's another *almost true* story by/about a real-life F-bomber to hammer it home.

Let's change my name to Geoff because it rhymes with 'deaf.' One day in this millennium, Geoff was busy doing what it is he loves doing. Since the birth of my little boy, I rarely get such a grand block of time to immerse myself in my hobby of hobbies. This was a good day (or night as it was). Sure it was raining outside and the streets were flooding the city over (or would that be under), but I was at home, safe and sound with my me-time.

My wife called and though she continued to ramble, I muted her existence. My little boy was in his bed sleeping, my wife was not there, and I was surfing the internet (what, that's a hobby). All was well. I soon said "I love you" and hung up the phone. Another hour passed. And then another. Where was my wife?

Had I listened, I would have learned that her car had been towed and that she was stranded downtown by herself. And she had no money to rescue the car from the city impound lot. Finally she called again. "Where are you!" we both screamed in unison. You can imagine what happened next. You guessed it, a lot of F-bombs lit up Ma Bell's ears.

From my other stories, you know that I am still together with my wife. I guess when I got her car out of jail, I was the hero (this is my only plausible explanation). But you will be happy to know that, for a time, we both refused to listen. So maybe we each actually demanded that things change, but neither one of us could hear the request.

Divide and Conquer

This concept has been around forever and has been used on battlefields and playgrounds all over the galaxy. It's a war strategy, and F-bombing is essentially being at war with oneself, so I don't think you can argue about its inclusion in this book. But as your partner is perhaps your ultimate opponent, I have decided to put it here in the marital massacre section. Has a certain ring to it, doesn't it?

Of course "divide and conquer," traditionally speaking, is the art of splitting up a larger, more powerful opponent into smaller bits for you to attack and destroy. And as marriages often result in split personalities and massive weight gain, this may be no small task. But we must get away from any physical attacks you may be envisioning and move under the skin. We must go into the biology of togetherness. It sounds scary, but I'm here to guide you.

The simplest forms to attack are the psyche and that emotional prison called the heart. Now before we get too deep, I am talking about the sie-key as a noun, not sike as a verb or expression. This is not something you say to your buddies after making them look stupid.

I've learned that partners get emotional about different things, but one thing that'll get them all fired up is bringing another lion into the den. I'm not talking about making cubs with that other lion or even getting all cat-nippy. That is too obvious. I'm talking about, well, talking.

All we have to do is confide in someone else (same sex as your partner works best). This is the time when we tell all about the issues we're having at home and then thank the other person for being such a good listener. It's simple, but extremely effective. This is dividing *yourself*, as you're sharing yourself with someone else, but it really shuts down your partner's heart, and we all know what that does to a person. I don't do this, but I have plenty of tear-soaked pillows from my dating life to know that it really works.

Another way to divide and conquer (on the psyche side) is to live as two instead of as one. What I mean by this is living like you're still single. When we went into the marriage, we had our own cars, our own bank accounts, our own credit cards, and our own paychecks. Of course I know we had a lot more stuff than that, but most of it is irrelevant now.

When first starting out in the marriage, we may keep this stuff separate until we get a-round to cutely adding each other to each other's stuff. My advice: keep stalling or put it off indefinitely. If something happens to your partner's car, he can get it fixed with money out of his paycheck. You see how this works? If your partner is running up her credit cards, then she can pay those off.

The reason this works is because as long as we keep everything separated, we have not fully committed to the relationship. I'm sure some of you think we have, but until we give someone the power to decimate our financial life, we haven't done jack. And if we are not financial F-bombers, then this may be terribly frightening for some of us.

Another road to Splitsville is dividing our time between our partner and our kids disproportionately. I hope that you know to spend more time with your kids on this one. Put them first, which as it turns out is a completely natural thing to do. This makes it that much more surreptitious. To save you from looking that freak word up, think secret agent man.

Our partners will see us as loving parents at first, which makes this one so darn good. But after seeing us living for the kids instead of the one who made the kids, an atomic wedgie will be driven between us and our significant others that will split us like the Grand Canyon. So if you're the sneaky type who still wants to look cool with the neighbors, this trick may be the one for you.

Since we're having so much fun, I thought I would throw in one more tactic. Someone probably does the bulk of the chores or maybe it is more equally split in your household. He does the cooking, she does the yard work, etc. Oh, did I get those backwards for most of you? Not if you're a grand F-bomber. This is the sneaky part of *Divide and Conquer*. The way it works is we say that the chores need to be split up because we're tired of doing the same old stuff (which actually may not be much of anything). But the key is that we want to do the other person's stuff. "Well, okay," our partners say, thinking full well that we're about to learn a valuable lesson.

Then we do things our way. If we start doing the laundry, we don't pay attention to hot or cold or darks or whites. We just stuff that hot mess in there and hit the go button. If we start mowing the lawn, we make up some crazy-ass patterns in the grass to bring out our artistic side. This dividing and conquering will drive the other person to heights of such unbridled anger that they may actually split us in two!

Here's another *almost true* story by/about a real-life F-bomber to hammer it home.

We will call her Kit because it rhymes with 'split.' Kit is a blonde bombshell, who, as it turns out, is from the same hometown as me. Kit is a smart girl who is a top seller for any company she works for. She is that good. It may be her looks, but either way, she gets some nice bonuses at the end of the year. Kit likes her bonuses. Kit also likes her Kit-time.

When Kit got married, she decided to keep the finances separate. She worked hard for her stuff, so she had her bank account, and her husband had his. The two were never to be mixed. She pays her car note, buys the groceries, and pays the bills, while he pays the mortgage and his car note. Kit is fair, and they each pay out roughly the same amount each month.

Mr. Kit is a good friend of mine. Mr. Kit and I

worked together and always made about the same amount of dough. But one day, Mr. Kit left me for another job, and now Mr. Kit's dough rises more than Kit's and mine combined. Kit thinks that maybe they should finally combine accounts, but Mr. Kit doesn't see why they should change now. He is fully enjoying the benefits of *Divide and Conquer*.

I warned Kit and Mr. Kit of the danger they're in because I want them to stay married (they throw awesome parties and still invite me to them). And while I may be an authority on F-bombing, they assure me that all is under control. They do agree that I am pretty messed up, though.

Be Somewhere Else

Being somewhere else is not to be confused with an aspect of refusing to listen, whereby we tune out and are only somewhere else in theory. I am ditching the abstract for something a little more concrete on this one. And note that I did not say be *someone* else. You're already married, so I just want you to be yourself—yes, *now* you can be yourself. But I really need for you to be somewhere else most of the time. Being somewhere else leads to speculation, accusation, and ultimately conflagration. We don't need no water, let the F-bomber burn!

This is a great tactic for all you overachievers out there. Why you? Because you're always on the go, looking for the next score. You're the ones who work all the time. And you never have time for anything else anyway.

But if you're like me and not an overachiever with a fat paycheck, maybe you should start spending more time at the J.O.B. You'll start to get noticed by the boss, you'll get a better office (or bigger cubicle), and you may even get your own parking space right next to the door so that you can get in there and start working sooner. Not to mention that all that success will surely make you more confident and appealing to partners everywhere. Or not.

Another great *Be Somewhere Else* place is the gym. We've got the membership, so we might as well put it to use. We don't even have to work out the whole time we're there. Take my lead and just sit around in that air conditioning, watching everyone else pull those muscles. Grab a protein bar, and by the time it takes to choke that sucker down, the gym will be closing up. Mission accomplished. Sure we could go home and do something with our partners, but then that's not being somewhere else, is it?

But the fun does not have to stop at work and the gym. Go get a hobby (clearly a multi-purpose technique) that gets you out of the house. And if you can do this stuff with some of your clients, then you've got a tax write-off. So the next time you see a Groupon that challenges you to be somewhere else, buy as many as you can. The F-bombing of your marriage may very well depend on it.

Here's another *almost true* story by/about a real-life F-bomber to hammer it home.

We will call him Vaughn because it rhymes with 'gone.' Vaughn is dead (obviously not me, although I've had dates tell me they wish I were dead). When he was alive, Vaughn was a real go-getter. He was married, had kids, had his own business, and was considered the king of *Be Somewhere Else*. He split his time between traveling the world, meeting with clients in bars, and home. Pretty much in that order. He put in a good 6-7 hours at home every day, most of which he used for belching and sleeping. The rest of the time he used to build his empire.

Successful? Yes, very much so. He made good money, experienced other cultures, got free booze from the tax system, and had a loving family. Vaughn kept this up for years, but with each year, he lost something. First it was his adventures, then it was his empire, then it was his family. He kept the social recreation for good measure. Vaughn lost everything, including the one thing that he thought he couldn't lose—his wife.

He F-bombed his marriage so well that the contract incinerated upon that final decree. Not even a trace was left to remind him of what had been. And all because he thought it wise to *Be*

Somewhere Else. And you thought this one was a lame duck. Au contraire fellow F-bombers. This is your secret weapon, your pièce de résistance! Bon appétit.

And for those of you with a morbid fascination, Vaughn died of natural causes (starvation). But I know it was losing everything that really did him in. Vaughn taught me that when a man has only food to fill his belly, he becomes a veil of humanity. But don't let this distract you from your purpose. Keep working yourself into the ground, so that your demise can be blamed on stress. It is not good for business when F-bombers actually kick the bucket, so heart attacks that serve to cover up the F-bombs are most welcome.

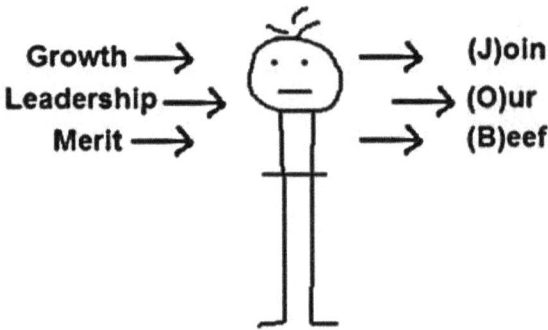

6

HOW TO F-BOMB YOUR CAREER

Intro

Since I've covered other important aspects of life, I thought I'd throw in the one that takes up most of our time. I work almost every day, and chances are that when I am not working, I am thinking about it in some way or another (whether it's dreading or dreaming to get back to it). Either way, work is substantial. Maybe it's because I get paid to do it or maybe it's because it's all I've got left thanks to my F-bombing everything else.

Let me make a distinction here, though. I am not referring to F-bombing our jobs. That takes very little effort (just ask any high-schooler). I'm talking about our careers. Just count the letters and you'll see that "career" is a much bigger, badder word. Careers have moxie, while jobs have time clocks. There's a big difference.

And F-bombing careers carries additional challenges such as dealing with massive legal and HR departments. These entities are in place to make F-bombing our careers something very difficult to do, as a solid case against us is often necessary to can our lazy butts.

F-bombing careers can be fairly easy for some jobbers who fell into careers. But what about the rest of us? With the guidelines set forth, it would take an idiot to promote us past our current stations (F-bombing our careers is sometimes more than a good, old-fashioned firing). It can be keeping us stuck in the same dingy place with no room to breathe.

Sound like you're already there? Well if so, congratulations. But I'm not giving you a pass on this chapter because when the old geezer down the hall finally retires and opens up that coveted office, you'll need to be aware of strategies in this chapter to keep you in your grungy Hell hole. So best of luck, and may you always have a job, even if you're saddled with a career.

Take it Personally

Have you ever seen a really good trial lawyer in action or even a child negotiating with her parents? Notice anything? Those making a good argument don't get their feathers ruffled. They present their ideas and remain cool like yesterday's vintage. Those who get all emotional lose.

Kids run off crying, parents are miserable, defendants go to jail, and trial lawyers get death threats instead of Christmas cards. What happened? What went wrong? Well, they took it personally.

If I don't get the raise I thought I deserved, I take it personally. If I'm passed over for a promotion, I take it personally. If the office temperature is too cold for my liking, I take it personally. If the copier ran out of paper AGAIN, I take it personally. See how easy it is? And more importantly, do you see how many opportunities there are to take things personally?

Believe it or not, when we take things personally, we act differently. And it shows. We wear our stress like bad breath—blaring to the world, but strangely silent to us. In short, it makes us snippy, and when we're overly snippy, people automatically think postal. Next thing you know, we've collected a few more complaints in our HR file. And all because someone drank all the coffee and didn't make another pot. So every time something like this happens, just say to yourself, "Oh, now it's personal!" and F-bomb away my loose-cannon friend.

Here's another *almost true* story by/about a real-life F-bomber to hammer it home.

We will call her Daisy because it rhymes with 'crazy.' Daisy was a nice girl (I'm obviously not

Daisy, but I am someone else in this story). Now Daisy had trouble making friends for some reason. Someone even tried to take Daisy under her wing to show her the ropes and give her a sliver of hope in the big, bad, corporate world. And another coworker noted the girl's meek manner and offered up some assertiveness training.

Now Daisy started to speak up. Daisy was coming into her own. She had a few faux friends and she was collecting some of that moxie that career people get as a bonus every year. Daisy was even given an extra duty that let her interact with the rest of the office. Things were looking up for Daisy and her career.

But one day, Daisy wanted to modify that extra assignment to be more in line with the way *she* wanted to do things. Not everyone agreed, though, as it complicated a system that had been in place for years. The new and improved Daisy didn't care. She remained assertive and stood her ground. And no one dared to challenge Daisy because she was a little off in the head, and they feared being shivved in a bathroom stall if they ever spoke out against her.

So no one challenged Daisy . . . except for CB (short for crazy bitch). Daisy took CB's stand against her personally. She raised her voice to CB, knowing that most times that's all it took to get her way. But CB yelled back. And a genuine cat fight occurred right there in the hall.

Daisy took each jab personally, while CB was

just being CB. In a matter of minutes, Daisy picked herself up and retreated to lick her wounds. After that day, Daisy got crazy, like have-to-put-her-down crazy. HR saved CB the trouble, and Daisy was eventually fired.

Daisy later wound up in jail for disorderly conduct. Now some will say that Daisy's brain was related to Abby Normal and that's why her career was F-bombed. But I say that she F-bombed her career by taking it personally. After all, look at the crazy people that we've worked with over the years. They're still employed aren't they? And some of them may even be your boss. Crazy has nothing to do with it, but it sure does make it entertaining.

Keep It to Yourself

I see this one all the time, and it makes me smile. When the boss people ask me to rank my value to the organization, I of course see myself as a vital asset. Why is this? Pride? Truth? Doesn't matter.

Now ask me if my current salary corresponds to my value to the company. Hmm. I of course think my pay for my vital services could be a little more robust. Why is this? Pride? Truth? Doesn't matter.

Now ask me how I can help the company grow to a bazillion-dollar juggernaut. Result? I ask if "bazillion" is a real word. Why is this? Pride? Truth? Now *this* matters! This is classic

Keep It to Yourself, and it's one of the most effective, if not *the* most effective, way to F-bomb your career. It's that good.

How many times have you been in a meeting where the boss asks a question to which no one gives an answer? Do you think everyone thought the question was rhetorical (i.e. not meant to be answered)? Or do you think that people actually had the answer, but given that it was so blatantly obvious, they refused to waste their breath on it? Either way, this is keeping it to yourself. By the way, management hates this!

Another way to keep it to yourself is seeing something that you know is wrong and just sweeping it under the rug (also called sticking your head in the sand). If I just walked into the break room and saw Harry and Sally reenacting a scene from *When Harry Met Sally*, what do I do? While it may be better to keep this one to myself, what if Harry and Sally were stealing chips out of the vending machine? Now *this* would be a dilemma. We're talking about breaking the law here. It gets tricky. If it ever came out that I saw the chip heist and kept it to myself, I too could be F-bombed—mission accomplished.

The last thing I'll comment on is complaining without offering solutions. We all think we have the right stuff and are vital to the organization, so we're obviously capable of providing an answer to a problem. But alas, we somehow never do. It's much easier to complain.

Complaining is linear; no outside-the-box thinking required. But complaining shows management that we're really only good for one thing. And to them, if we're only good for one thing, then we should be paid like we're only good for one thing. So if you've got an idea of how things could be better, just keep it to yourself and instead complain about it. Then just for fun, see how long it takes for everyone else to catch up to your genius.

Here's another *almost true* story by/about a real-life F-bomber to hammer it home.

We will call him Mitch because it rhymes with 'bitch.' Mitch is a hard worker, and he has hard worker friends (you got it, I'm not Mitch). And when these hard workers get together to gossip around the office, they always talk about how much better they are than everyone else. Well one day, Mitch and a little hard worker buddy were shooting their mouths off about how easy their boss had it, and how an idiot could do his job. What they didn't realize was that Boss Man was behind them and heard everything. But Boss Man didn't take it personally; he just filed the information away for a later time.

Well, it wasn't long until Boss Man had to go to a big, important meeting with other boss people. Boss Man couldn't have things fall through the cracks, so he picked someone to take over as boss man until he returned. Without hesitation, Boss Man told Mitch that he thought Mitch was ready to be in charge. And if things went well, then perhaps Mitch was due for a promotion. And if things went poorly . . . well, there was no sense in discussing that because Boss Man's job wasn't that hard.

Mitch ran and told Little Hard Worker Buddy all about his new status. Little Hard Worker Buddy thought he'd get a promotion too, after Mitch moved Boss Man off his perch. Mitch and Little Hard Worker Buddy went out for drinks that night to celebrate.

The next day, Mitch's phone rang more than usual. And problems surfaced. And business would be lost if Mitch didn't handle them quickly. Mitch yelled at people. Mitch wanted answers. But everyone was too entrenched in *Keep It to Yourself*.

Mitch panicked. Mitch lost business. Mitch was almost fired. Mitch learned a valuable lesson. *Keep It to Yourself* is a great way to F-bomb a career. Mitch and Little Hard Worker Buddy are no longer friends. Mitch learned another valuable lesson. These F-bomb techniques can move over to other areas of your life. Thank you, Mitch, for showing us the way!

Keep It Fair

I'm not talking about your golf game here, although I can see the merits of hitting your shots down the middle to make your boss despise you. Instead, I'm referring to the notion that everything should be fair and just. I know it may be hard to wrap your mind around this one, but it is a subtle trick to F-bomb your career.

Watch kids on a playground and eventually you'll hear "that's not fair!" One kid takes another kid's ball—that's not fair! Now watch those kids when they start to play sports in high school. Star athlete kid gets a scholarship to play football—that's not fair? Lines start to blur as the kids get older. Only when dealing with young kids does the fair rule make any sense.

Let's shift to adults now. The rules start to bend—a lot. Take my favorite pro football team. I'd be pretty upset if the coach benched the star running back to let the punter give it a go for a while. Why? Because these are adults with careers. There's no such thing as fair anymore. And the same is true with office workers.

Just as in sports, this brand of "fair" doesn't belong in the workplace; it's a childish notion that we slackers use to stay in the game. *Keep It Fair* only serves to show how different I am from the leaders of the company. It shows them that the rut I'm in is exactly where I want to be. I am an adult with a career, acting like a child with a job—F-bombing it all.

Most leaders know there's no such thing as fair. It's a crazy story that we tell ourselves. The idea of fair breeds mediocrity. Hint: we want to be in this happy place. It keeps the cream from rising to the top. I once heard a quote to support the absurdity of fairness—"it's like not expecting a bull to charge you because you're a vegetarian." F-bombers live in absurdity by the way.

So if you get more money than everyone else at work, please make it public knowledge. And call it out if you get a promotion and no one else does. And of course do the same thing when it comes to raises. *Keep It Fair* my friend.

Here's another *almost true* story by/about a real-life F-bomber to hammer it home.

We will call her Claire because it rhymes with 'fair.' Claire's a manager, one of the ring leaders chosen to tame the animals (I'm one of the animals by the way). But one has to wonder how far up the circus ladder Claire can climb. Why? Because Claire believes in fair. That's right, some management still believes in this cotton-candy-dream. For day-to-day activities, it isn't necessarily a bad thing. But throw money into the ring, and the lions get restless.

Now Claire is blessed with an awesome staff, all experts in their fields. Her team draws a crowd and has the best opening acts in the business. Of course Claire wants to keep her team happy, because as any good boss knows, the right team makes her circus life that much more enjoyable.

Claire knows from personal experience that

money talks and poverty walks. So when it came time for reviews, Claire wanted to be fair and give everyone the same bonus and raise. And while this sounded good to the bearded lady whose act didn't do so well last year, those other top performers didn't like this approach so much.

The lion tamer and the magician wanted their just rewards and felt that the bearded lady should've adapted her act to bring home more bacon. They didn't like someone taking a few strips off their plates to fill hers, especially since she was clearly on a diet. They let Claire know exactly how they felt. Claire got upset. She was only trying to be fair. But as there is no such thing as fair, some of those top performers had to now consider other options. And no matter what they decided, Claire had lost, for a moment, an edge that she once had.

Claire kept it fair. Poor Claire. She was unaware. Those who walked on air, are they still there? They went where? A team disbanded over being fair? Gone is the flair. Say a prayer for Claire. I dare say make it fair. But beware. Make it too fair and you may lose earnings per share. And that is F-bombing your career, so steer clear my dear, if to F-bombing, you don't adhere.

Health

7

HOW TO F-BOMB YOUR HEALTH

Intro

"At least you've got your health!" It's kind of an insult, really. It means my friends think I have absolutely nothing else going for me. It's sad. And what's even sadder is that we don't all have our health. Some of us are so F-bomb-ridden that it's a miracle we're still around. This is a true testament to how durable our bodies really are. And this makes F-bombing our health somewhat of a mystery.

I've brought you surefire ways that have torn my body down to nothing, and I've stayed away from the obvious methods like smoking, drinking, drugging, and toddler-licking everything in sight. We all see enough of that stuff at home and don't need to explore it any further. So give this chapter a read because you've always got your health . . . as miserable as it may be.

Don't Rest for Nuthin'

I'm busy, whether it's going to work, going to school, or just sitting around watching my morning game shows. I know that life slows down for no one. And if life's gonna play hard ball with me, then maybe I should return the favor. So let's draw a line in the sand and tell life we don't rest for nuthin'!

When I *Don't Rest for Nuthin'*, I'm telling my life (i.e. my health) to stick it. Sure, it may take a while, but if I maintain that frenetic pace, then I'll incapacitate myself in no time. I just can't give in to life telling me to rest. This is the F-bombing devil talking. So I tell him to get his charred butt in line with the rest of them, 'cause I don't rest for nuthin'.

And I can play this scenario out in a number of ways. For instance, you know that email that just came in? What am I waiting for? I need to jump on it. And when the next one comes in, I'll repeat. It's that simple. It's the reason my work gave me a smartphone in the first place. So be Mr. Accessible like me, and let's hop to it!

Just destroyed a workout? Don't rest now! Hit it again tomorrow, or better yet, do two-a-days. Let's burn those calories until our bodies become their own Halloween costumes. Rest is for sissies. So play hard because there is no rest in the world of F-bombing your health. Now I *Don't*

Rest for Nuthin' for the simple reason of not even having my health. I need something in my life, so I might as well get back to work!

Here's another *almost true* story by/about a real-life F-bomber to hammer it home.

We will call her Lizzy because it rhymes with 'busy.' Lizzy's a classic overachiever (not me), signing up for everything! She can't say no. Classroom mom at school? Check. Devoted wife? Check. Super mom? Check.

Are we playing chess? We have a lot of checks, but no checkmates. But don't you worry. Things are starting to slip for Lizzy. She's not as quick as she once was. She's growing more tired by the day. She's starting to look beyond her years. The solution? Well, Lizzy thinks it's more work, that she needs to crank things up and reignite the fire. And she's right. I know it, you know it, and F-bombers everywhere know it.

But I don't think she wants to be an F-bomber. Should I tell her? Would she even listen? Well, I told her. She didn't listen. Secretly, I think she wants to be more like us F-bombers, which would mean that she actually did listen, and that she's right on plan. Or maybe she's an F-bomber because she didn't listen. Still, Lizzy is slowing down (even though she's speeding up). Soon, it will be checkmate for old Lizzy, and her king of health will be laid to rest.

Rush Right In

Rushing right in precludes thought. It's what I've done when I thought I actually had a chance with a girl. So I'm not referring to rushing right in to burning buildings. While that may prove extremely dangerous to your health, it's too closely linked to heroism. F-bombers are a lot of things, but "hero" is typically not one of them.

And please don't confuse this technique with the former *Don't Rest for Nuthin'*. Those F-bombers rush around like starved vegetarians at the all-you-can-eat salad bar. *Rush Right In* has nothing to do with salad or bars. It's about getting after it—in the moment, not every moment.

So let's explore rushing right in, as it relates to health. Ever see the emergency room on weekends? Packed . . . with people just like me. Why are they there? Besides of course to seal up those chinks in the armor? Hint: when I lead you in like this, just blurt out the title of the section. That's right! They rushed right in! Why else would they jump off the roof into a hot tub? (I've done this by the way, and it is critical to stick the landing).

As a fun exercise for you and your crew, that is if you haven't F-bombed your social life yet, go to the ER and chat up the folks you see in there. You'll find some of the best *Rush Right In* examples on the planet, and you may even learn a few tricks to try your own. Warning: Do not laugh in their faces though, unless it is clear that they'll be alright after a few thousand dollars and months of rehab. Otherwise, you just may be joining them overnight. This will be costly, and there are far better ways to F-bomb your finances than getting put in the ER by someone who accidentally ran over his toe with a lawnmower.

If rushing right in doesn't seem like it's your thing, just give me a minute. Have you ever had something go wrong whereby the cure was rest? I've needed rest for Montezuma's Revenge, the flu, turf toe, and even heartache. But I treat just enough to get me back to around 50%, and then I rush right in to whatever it is that I do. This has been so detrimental to my health that it has kept me feeling miserable and altogether useless for much longer than normal. That's exponential F-bombing.

Here's another *almost true* story by/about a real-life F-bomber to hammer it home.

We'll change my name to Murray because it rhymes with 'hurry.' Murray is not the rush-right-in-to-a-bar-fight kind of guy. I'm really not even a bar kind of guy. I'm not a do-nothinger either. But what I do is rush right in.

I like goals. Can't say that I'm an overachiever, though, because I never really achieve anything. I'm just an average achiever. But average achievers are prime rush-right-inners. We think a little, but not too much. We're active, but not too active. We're smart, but not too smart.

One day, I decided to try to get on a reality show, and I knew that I needed to be in better shape. Now from my pattern, you might guess that I'm in shape, but not in too good of shape. When the weather turned nice, I decided to go out for a run. So I did. Life was good. But running like a first-grader was boring, so I decided to spice it up along the way with some push-ups (you never know who's waiting to be impressed).

All was good . . . until I stood up. That's right, folks. All I had to do was stand up. Bam! My calf ruptured, and I was a long way from home on a dirt trail to nowhere. I still to this day don't walk right. And I'm scared to death to run (unless being chased by first-graders).

See how easy it is? If I had warmed up, I probably would've been fine, but that's not the F-bombing way. I learned that rushing right in takes no thought at all and is easy enough for anyone to do. We need these examples. If you need more, go to the ER. You just may see me there.

Go Get Your Fast Food Fix

This is something I used to say to those people on the road in front of me swinging in for fries and slowing up traffic, and this topic is more of an homage than anything else (as it should be painfully obvious). I now get my fast food fix for one of three reasons. One: I can't afford a decent meal; Two: I'm jonesing for some good old-fashioned grease; or Three: I don't have time to eat properly (my favorite). I don't care which camp you're in, although if you make it a habit of getting your fast food fix, you may be in D-camp. And as luck would have it, D-camp leads to dehydration, which is also excellent for F-bombing your health. So no worries.

Here's another *almost true* story by/about a real-life F-bomber to hammer it home.

We will call him Matt because it rhymes with 'saturated fat.' Matt's always had an issue with weight (not me, I'm a 90 lb weakling). Matt loves fine dining. Matt's not too good for a fast food fix, though. Matt's a good cook. Matt even cooks food so that it tastes like fast food. See anything wrong with this? Neither do I.

Matt is F-bombing his health and being an example to us all. We should thank Matt. Matt has a few health problems—he's on the verge of fatabetes. There is a piece of Matt that wants to get healthy, but Matt still gets his fast food fix.

Have you ever known getting your "fix" to be healthy? Me neither. "Fix" indicates "broken." These F-bombers fight against healthy eating at every turn, no matter which First Lady is leading the charge against their fast food ways. And they are paving the way for the rest of us to have more air to breathe in the long run. They are true humanitarians, full of self-sacrifice. So the next time you see people who don't know what to do with their lives, just tell them with a smile, "*Go Get Your Fast Food Fix!*"

Live for Moderation

You may be thinking, *This is not F-bombing! This is trickery. You've given us a way to be healthy!* Well, you're right. It is trickery. But I'm not the one doing the tricks. It's the medical community and every other self-proclaimed picture of health. "Everything in moderation," they say. "A little here and there won't hurt you." Are they kidding? I'm here to set the record straight.

Could it be that this moderation ploy was actually established by doctors who were too afraid to tell us to stop what we're doing altogether? They feared anarchy, revolution, chaos. In short, they didn't believe in us. This is probably where the old "four out of five doctors" statement came from. That one guy actually thought we could do it. Yes, that was a big mistake for his career and his social life. (He is now an undercover F-bombing consultant.)

Just because doctors were able to show that, in moderation, some pretty nasty stuff could be used for good (think venom for antivenin) doesn't mean that this applies to everything.

Use a different snake venom, and we're as dead as that argument's about to be. Same principle applies to vaccines. And to have these vaccines and antivenins work, we have to have the foreign agent enter our bodies!

Now, consider all those things that we do in moderation. Smoking, drinking, recreational drugs, food that falls under Section 1 of the Five Second Rule. Are these things used to combat some foreign agent that's penetrated our bodies (stay focused, Giggles)? No, probably not. What we've actually done is put the poison into our body *on purpose.*

This moderation stuff just doesn't work, unless of course you're an F-bomber. Drinking kills brain cells. You don't grow new ones. When you smoke, you damage your lungs. You don't grow new ones. So you see, moderation is F-bombing us all over the place, doing way more damage than we ever imagined.

You just gotta love it when society sets us up for F-bombing our lives. One has to wonder if those "everything in moderation" rule-makers are following their own advice or if they are waiting for us to become dependent on their services. Wow, that's actually genius.

Here's another *almost true* story by/about a real-life F-bomber to hammer it home.

We will call her Britt because it rhymes with

'little bit.' Britt is short for Brittney which rhymes with 'little bitchy,' and this so describes Britt when she doesn't live for moderation. Britt's not exactly an abstinence junkie, and she's not yet a junkie junkie, so she really needs her moderation. Moderation is her golden ticket to freedom. It's like a free hall pass to do whatever she wants . . . and all because society has told her to live for moderation.

One night, she decided to have moderation on an empty stomach. As you know, the body treats this type of moderation as a full out binge. So what is moderation for some (staying within legal limits) can be jail time for others. Luckily for Britt, she has a lot of friends who stay sober enough to drive her home. But unlucky for Britt's shiny new car, vomit down the side of a car door being smeared at 50 mph turns into concrete chaos. The smell does keep carjackers away, but unfortunately for Britt, it keeps everyone else away too.

You've gotta love it when a good F-bombing is so multi-purpose, though. So go forth and keep living for moderation. Society wants it this way. Don't disappoint society . . .

Swim in Denial River

I like to swim. Do you like to swim? Have you ever swam in a river? Well, if you have, you know that rivers move. And even if the current looks smaller than sparrow spittle, chances are it can carry you away, and it damn sure won't let you get anywhere if you try to swim against it. Denial is a lot like that.

A philosopher once said that we can never step in the same river twice. If you disagree, then let me explain it this way, which is the way he would explain it if he were here and spoke good English. Rivers are constantly in a state of flux, always moving, always changing, each drop of water only being but a small instant at our feet before moving past our awareness. Therefore, the river is never the same, even moment to moment. So it is therefore impossible for us to step in the same river twice, which is a good thing because people like me pee in rivers when we've really got to go.

The point of that river discussion is to let you know that the river is never what you think it is because it's always changing (thank God). We are like the river. We are never who we think we are (and not nearly as good as we give ourselves credit for being). To support your F-bombing ways though, I hope you don't believe that last statement, because if you believe it, then you realize that there is room for improvement, and it's *not* believing that speaks to your denial, and you know what that leads to.

When I really think I know all there is to know about myself, I am apt to relax when it comes to taking care of myself. I'll have the tendency to rationalize what's best for me and what I can handle or get away with doing. I'll use this so-called knowledge as a floatation device and may even stop swimming altogether. And that's when my inner F-bombs go off, sinking me to the bottom of the river along with my health.

That nagging pain in my side that must have come from those jalapeños I just ate never gets looked at. That headache I've been getting because I've been stressed lately gets little more than a few Advil thrown its way. And those dizzy or fainting spells are blamed on lack of food. Before I know it, I find myself fighting to breathe my last breath. All because I've been swimming in denial river. What I have today is easily taken tomorrow . . . by the river.

Here's another *almost true* story by/about a real-life F-bomber to hammer it home.

We will call him Raine because it rhymes with 'pain.' Raine was full of life (that puts me out of it). He always knew what he wanted. Raine was one of those guys everybody liked. He had all the answers and was happy to share them with anyone who would listen.

One day, Raine had a little stomach discomfort. He said it was indigestion. This went on for a while until the pain got so bad that he had to admit that he didn't know what was wrong. He went to the doctor. He got some tests done. And then the prognosis came. Four months, give or take. To live. To prepare. To die.

Raine did what he could to treat his aggressor. And low and behold, he beat the four months. But Raine died anyway. He swam in denial river and it killed him. It's easy to drown in denial, never admitting our faults. This makes us weak, real F-bombers. I liked Raine. I just wish he knew about the river. But for some reason, strong swimmers never listen.

I'm no longer a true fan of F-bombing your health because I'm a wimp and I don't like its painful result. So why mention it? So that you can decide if F-bombing your health is truly something you want to do; it's not something to take lightly. But rest assured, the methods outlined here (no matter how benign they may seem) can tear you down. People F-bomb their health because they think 60, 70, or 80 is long enough to live . . . that is until they reach 60, 70, or 80.

Family

Birthdays → → TV
Holidays → → TV
Weddings → → TV

8

HOW TO F-BOMB YOUR FAMILY

Intro

Family. We've all got 'em, like it or not. Some are better than others, but I have learned that all of them are pretty whacked out—no matter how pristine they appear. Families are rich with traditions and have more skeletons in the closet than I've had rejections. They have so many secrets that they make the CIA look like Camp Fire Girls. On the surface they're covertly normal, but we mustn't forget that they invented disorder and chaos and altogether kooky. And if you've been slighted one too many times at Thanksgiving dinner, you just may be up for F-bombing your family.

These methods will show you how to make sociopaths out of your kids and ruin what unity you have left. I have not included those methods related specifically to spouses, as marriage has its own glorious chapter in this book. Now read up; another holiday is just around the corner. Family time is coming.

Abuse Substance

No, I didn't mean substance abuse, even though hanging out with my derelict family has forced me to consider such in years past. The only thing that truly holds a family together is substance, that is, all the stuff that's real, that has meat to it. It's the true meaning, no smoke, no mirrors. So it stands to reason that to F-bomb your family is to abuse substance.

Abusing substance is multi-layered. It could be as simple as lying about an event. For example, I took the last cookie, but instead of fessing up, I blame my sister. That's abusing substance. It could be taking truth and using it to impose your will. For example, I caught my sister sneaking into the house at three o'clock in the morning, so I tell her that unless she does what I say, I'll expose her curfew crusade. This is abusing substance. It could even be using truth as a weapon. For example, my sister gets busted for smoking dope, so I bring this up for the rest of her life to prove what a loser she is—abusing substance.

So you see, abusing substance is very powerful. It can literally tear families apart. Most families already implement this tradition without even thinking about it. Maybe it's one of those family heritage things, and maybe it's why so many families are jackpot crazy. I don't know all the answers, but I do know that it only takes one or two family members to affect the whole family. Now that's crazy good stuff.

Here's another *almost true* story by/about a real-life F-bomber to hammer it home.

We will call him Gene because it rhymes with 'mean.' Gene was one mean SOB (not me, but I am in this story). He abused substance like nobody's business while doing a little substance abuse on the side. Truly talented was Gene. One night, Gene came home and made up a story about where he'd been. When Gene was called out for lying, he then proceeded to threaten his family with a few truths he did have. Gene had been in this same pattern for years, and his son grew tired of Gene's F-bombing ways.

Gene mouthed off to his son in grand fashion, abusing substance with every syllable. But on this particular night, Sonny Boy wasn't having it. Sonny Boy said that the abuse was going to end right then and there. Gene didn't appreciate being challenged under his own roof, so he told Sonny Boy to give it his best shot. Sonny Boy thought better of it, but Gene couldn't help but abuse substance with his mom and sis too.

Sonny Boy's fist crashed into Gene's chest

with a big thwack, and Gene went tumbling over the back of the couch. Mom and Sis looked on in horror. Sonny Boy stood there thinking that he didn't hit Gene that hard because he knew for a fact that he hit like a girl. Sonny Boy then realized that abusing substance must hollow out a man.

The family went off to their respective rooms, leaving Gene on the floor to wallow in his substance. A divorce was coming. From his wife. From his daughter. And from Sonny Boy.

Families can deal with substance abuse, but abusing substance is crossing the line. So if you want an effective way to F-bomb your family, consider this gem from the vault.

Fret About It

Fretting is serious business. Just look it up in the dictionary if you want a little dimension. It's like acid on the family jewels. Yet I've never met a family who doesn't fret about something.

So who are the worry warts in your family? You? Your mother? Your crazy cousin? Well, whoever they are, you should give them a big ol' hug for F-bombing the family for you. It gives you time to go F-bomb something else. But if no one is fulfilling this role, then it's up to you.

So why is it so important? Fretting is self-destructive, which inevitably takes energy away from the whole family. The fretter is a weak link in an already twisted chain of DNA. All that fretting gradually tears down the fretter. And as this role is usually taken by the caregivers, F-bombing the self becomes F-bombing the family.

Fretting is also tied to trust. Fretters find it difficult to trust themselves and others. They say things like, "I trust you, but I don't trust everyone else." This creates distance, and distance creates seeing each other once a year at either Christmas or Thanksgiving.

So until fretting becomes an Olympic sport like trampoline jumping, no one will respect the fretter. Fretting gets old to the rest of the family too. Fretters create unnecessary work for everyone because the family has to find ways to comfort the fretter. This fretter role should already be taken, but if it's not, just *Fret About It*.

Here's another *almost true* story by/about a real-life F-bomber to hammer it home.

We will call her Jess because it rhymes with 'stress.' Jess is now an old woman, worrying about old woman things. But when she was younger, she was the family fretter. If we were five minutes late, she put her fret expression on and wore it well after we finally came home. If dinner time was an hour away, she fretted about what to make. If no one ate what she cooked, she fretted about them going hungry.

Jess became so good at fretting that other parents asked her what *they* should worry about. Jess could fret about things that could physically never happen unless gravity stopped working. She was that good. Everyone probably thought her name was Jess Fretter. But all that fretting pushed her family into lying about their goings on.

Now Jess had one wild child on her hands, and fretting was not the right approach for keeping her in check. It got to where Wild Child said one thing and did the exact opposite. Jess still fretted more than ever, even if that which was said (i.e. the lie) was of little consequence. Jess pushed Wild Child further and further away with all that fretting, until one day Wild Child was gone for good. Then Jess really started to fret. Jess was on the edge of a nervous breakdown. But don't worry, she lied to the rest of her family so they wouldn't fret about it.

Get Your Glow Tan On

Unfortunately for tanning centers everywhere, I am not advocating using their services. And I'm not speaking of what you may look like after engaging in certain activities, especially as this is in the family section. I'm referring to sticking your face in front of those glowy electronic devices that make your life so much more fun than it was back in the 80's and 90's.

Smartphones, tablets, iPods, gaming devices, TVs, and e-readers were invented so that we would not have to waste another minute listening to our parents relive the same stories they've been telling us since we learned to listen. But even moms and dads are getting in on the action now. They may say that it's only to keep up with us, but it's so they won't have to interact with each other.

Statistics tell us that this is an effective method for F-bombing your family. If you look at the divorce rate statistics, you will see that the rates increase drastically from around 1950-1980. And then they start to level off and even decline toward the present day. What changed? Well to start, it was in the 80's when more people had TVs in the home. Granted, they were as big as hybrids, but people had them. Can you say *Get Your Glow Tan On*?

So it appears that in the years since 1980, a time when the glow makers have increased exponentially, families are more apt to stay together, even though they may have more disdain for each other than ever before. Is glow tanning numbing the senses so that families can wallow in their misery for longer periods of time?

While this may be good for improving divorce rates, it's absolutely crushing the family dynamic. When no one pays attention to each other, love and respect start to die off. So, if you're up for F-bombing your family, *Get Your Glow Tan On*. Now get out there and neglect your family!

Here's another *almost true* story by/about a real-life F-bomber to hammer it home.

We will call her Joanne because it rhymes with 'glow tan.' Joanne is a girl who loves her phone. She texts, she checks in, she tweets, she surfs, she updates, she photographs, she shares. She does this constantly. It is so bad (or should I say good) that her online friends know more about what she's doing than her own family knows.

Joanne burns along, oblivious to the chasm she's creating between herself and her family. She thinks she's living, when in effect, she's dying. She has everything she claimed she always wanted: husband, kids, house, car, career. Of course that list never included a phone. She never wanted a phone to make her happy, but it turns out in the end, that's all she really needs.

Joanne's husband and kids have noticed her love affair with her phone. But, they don't like playing seconds to anyone or anything. They have yet to tell Mom this, as they think she should inherently know this. But when she reads the email one of them tells me he's about to send, or she sees a relationship status change online, she will finally realize what she has—a phone and 1700 friends to tell her it'll be okay. I wonder if any of them are closet F-bombers wondering if she got her glow tan on. This insider knows, but will everyone else?

Fahgetta Bout It

I'm asked all the time to pick up something on my way home. And occasionally I forget. I'm a pretty busy person who can barely keep track of my own junk, much less someone else's. Still, family members continue to ask me to do things for them. It could be as harmless as taking out the trash, or it could be as dire as picking up little Timmy's medication so that he can make it through the night. The bottom line is that they shouldn't be counting on me for anything. But that's what families do—count on each other.

One way to get them to stop asking is to *Fahgetta Bout It*. If I do this enough, I will move into worthless, good-for-nothing status. That's utopia for F-bombers by the way. The message we send our families is that we just don't care about them. And the beauty of this technique is that even if we don't do it on purpose, it is construed as if we did.

Dejected family members (if they have any fight left in them) will say things like, "If I'm important to you, then you'd remember!" And if they're really riled up, they may even give an example, and you know how much I adore a good example. Does this sound familiar to you (you know I've heard it)? "If not remembering something would actually kill you, do you think you'd remember it then?" Yeah, I'd remember it because I'd tattoo it on my face! But putting "Pick up eggs and kitty litter" on my face isn't exactly tattoo worthy.

And don't think that *Fahgetta Bout It* just relates to everyday chores and favors. We can use it to forget about birthdays, anniversaries, your kids' soccer games, and any other big-time event. The bigger the better of course, as it has a more penetrating impact. A few of these doozies can be like forgetting a hundred chores. These are like knock-out punches. You set up the family with all those *Fahgetta Bout It* jabs, and then, wham, you totally hose your wife on her birthday or miss your kid's graduation. You will be talked about in every mom's group in town. And you *will* be compared to other F-bombers in your hood, so be sure to blow it out and represent.

Here's another *almost true* story by/about a real-life F-bomber to hammer it home.

We will call him Javier because it rhymes with 'not a care.' Javier is a salesman. He stays pretty busy. He serves his clients well. Too well. They take a lot of Javier's time, so that when he gets a break, he likes to relax. Relaxing does not include chores.

Javier is married. His wife stays at home. She asks Javier to pick stuff up on his way home from the office. Javier does this 25% of the time. His wife fusses at him when he forgets. She says he forgets because he doesn't love her anymore.

This has been going on for years. And while the quality of their life is fair at best, they will always be together. You see, Javier is very good looking (not me, as I look like a pogo stick with hair) and very good at other things. Mrs. Javier is not willing to give that up. So their marriage will continue as is until one of them dies. Not bad, but not great. It is what it is.

Not all these stories end up with the F-bombers on top (or would that be the bottom)? With Javier and Mrs. Javier, I don't think it matters. But this story should tell you something. If you are good looking, then you just may have to work a little harder to F-bomb your life. This is a universal truth that not even I can change. That's why I present you with so many methods to get the job done.

So if you're mirror-challenged like me, then this could be a piece of cake for you, as long as you have a terrible personality to go along with it. Again, I understand that this is a rare bird, and again, this is why I give you all the examples. Now *Fahgetta Bout It* and move along.

Religion

9

HOW TO F-BOMB YOUR RELIGION

Intro

Oh no you didn't. But yes, of course I did. Religion is a part of life just like marriage, family, health, et.al. And before you tell me that you don't have religion, you had better think again. We all have religion. It may be nontraditional, but I'm willing to bet that we've all formed a system of beliefs about life and the world around us. And I'm also willing to bet that those beliefs are not our own, but instead belong to a world of people with the same views as us. In essence, that is religion. It is your religion.

So whether you believe in God, gods, spirits, witchcraft, Dungeons and Dragons, or Darwin, you have religion. And there are some people who like to F-bomb your religion, as I've witnessed with my own eyes. I'm no longer one of these people, but I've employed some of these techniques in the past and know they work. So in the spirit of wholeness, I bring to you these methods.

As there are literally thousands of religions, I cannot come up with ways to F-bomb them all. If I don't get yours, I apologize, but I hope you do understand the difficulty and even the danger of presenting such information. Depending on your beliefs, you could lose your soul, your status in the afterlife, or your Starbucks privileges in certain states. So tread lightly my fellow F-bombers. This is right up there with F-bombing education. So if you're in doubt here, it's probably one area better left to the professionals bent on complete self-annihilation.

And one more thing: people who F-bomb their religion don't like to admit it, so I will not be telling their stories or mine. Besides, I don't want to be damned for throwing them under the bus if it was not their religion's plan for them. Confession is their burden to carry, whether they want to admit it or not.

Just Sit Back and Listen

Most religions have an official manual or doctrine to go by. And a lot of these were written way back when English wasn't even a second language offered in schools. Therefore, the translations get a little questionable by today's standards. It's like they're speaking in riddles or something. And if you're not good at riddles, then these manuals can be a little tiresome.

So what do we do? Well, lucky for us, most religions have a head honcho that can answer all our questions. They even give these people their own offices and all sorts of free stuff. These people read the manual and translate it for us.

So just sit back and listen to these experts. They can help out tremendously. But why in all that's holy/unholy (according to your religion) would this be F-bombing our religion? The key is in the first word of the section title: *Just*, as in *only*. Turns out this is dangerous. The very facet of religion that makes it fit like your favorite pair of jeans is that you should be able to study it for yourself and then ask questions as needed. Religion speaks to us if we want it to.

Never has lightning struck my butt more often than when I've just sat back and listened. When I just sit back and listen, I'm only getting the story that the expert wants me to hear, the story that was right for *him*. Now if he was truly called to speak to me, then I'd be in business, but I'm still expected to learn it for myself because it may be *me* who is the one to be called on to speak to him.

This method of just sitting back and listening includes more than just the expert, but everyone, and lucky for us again, everyone has something to say. But only the fool believes everything people tell him. He just sits back and listens; he doesn't challenge; he doesn't learn. Most religions don't like foolish behavior, so to

F-bomb those religions, *Just Sit Back and Listen*.

Straddle that Fence

Fences separate one side from another. They clearly state what is mine and what is my neighbor's. Fences set boundaries. People usually don't like me crossing their boundaries. And religions, being made up of a whole bunch of people, are the same way.

Jumping the fence is considered trespassing. That's illegal and punishable in most states. And lawbreakers and religions typically don't do well together. But I'm not talking about jumping the fence here. I want you to straddle that fence.

Straddling the fence is a much more egregious assault. Hard to fathom, but it is. If you study enough doctrines and manuals which give the bylaws and holidays for particular religions, you'll see that I speak truth, which is definitely hard to discern among thousands of religions. But why is straddling the fence so wrong?

Are you a decisive person? Lean more toward indecision? We're all indecisive at times (unless you are a truly gifted F-bomber with no moral compass whatsoever). But think about the process you go through when you're making a decision. Should I or shouldn't I? If I say yes, then the world will end, but if I say no, I won't get what I want. And while we're trying to make up our minds as to which flavor of ice cream we'll have, someone invariably screams, "Will you just pick something already!" And there you have it.

Do you think your god, frog prince, elfin troll (or whoever it is you worship), likes indecision? Especially when it comes to them? They want us on their side of the fence with both feet, looking over at the other side giving them the evil eye and singing spirit songs. I've even seen it written that it's better to choose the wrong side than to never choose a side at all. It brings new meaning to "shit or get off the pot." So if you want to F-bomb your religion, stay constipated, and by all means, *Straddle that Fence.*

Heal Thyself

I almost included this in the health section, but the whole thyself thing forced my hand. Divine intervention? I don't know, but I'm too scared to turn back now. So let's talk about healing thyself.

Heal Thyself is another one of those multidimensional topics. Firstly, it speaks to our healing ourselves. But to peel the onion a little further, it specifically speaks to our healing ourselves. Yes, I realize I just said that, but this one is hard to get. I will say it another way and peel that onion a little further. It *definitely* speaks to our healing ourselves. Did the emphasis help?

It's like this. Every time we peel an onion, we

get to another layer. But it is still an onion. It is an onion all the way down. We are the onion in *Heal Thyself*. It is all us. Nothing else. This is in direct contrast to most religions. Most religions consider themselves more than *just* us. That religion's higher power does the healing. We're just an onion. But when we heal thyself, we become the higher power, and we come dangerously close to F-bombing our religion. I'll admit that we can have the higher power dwell within us, but if we find ourselves taking the credit, then we should high-five our egos because we are probably F-bombing our religion.

I realize this technique is very deep and may require rereading a few times. Sometimes F-bombing is not as easy as we'd like it to be, especially where religion is concerned. It's like we have to fight a higher power or something, and that's exhausting.

Tell a Story

People have been telling stories since time began, and it's how we've gotten to where we are today. And we all love a good story. But unfortunately, good stories have become rife with "Oh no he didn't!" And it's these elements that tend to get us into trouble when we go all religion.

You may have heard that there is a time and a place for everything, and storytelling is no different. This may come as a shocker, but most religions would have us focus on other things besides updating our fellow devotees on the latest divorces in the congregation. These same religions take a stand for truth (whatever that actually looks like), and we could be telling 100% of the truth without a single embellishment. Still, we would be F-bombing our religion. It may not be fair to some, but it is what it is.

It all goes in line with the spirit of whatever is being said. And no matter how we spin it and try to defend our position, telling stories in the religion arena is just not a good thing. It is F-bombing and highly frowned upon. So if this is your mission, then by all means, go tell a story.

Play for the Other Team

You know how you feel when one of the star players on *your* team hightails it for another team? One day we're cheering at how awesome this guy is, and the next minute we're calling him every name in the book. It's nothing personal, but the guy becomes a traitor overnight. Well, religions are a lot like us in this scenario, especially when we decide to go play for the other team.

People feel duped when we change religions. They wonder if we were ever really part of the team. They gave us their playbook. They invited us to their picnic socials. And they took our donations for all the good work they were doing.

Why the betrayal? Why the hatred?

This will force our old religion to do one of three things: let us go and treat us as an outcast for the rest of our lives; try to win us back with a better offer, inviting us to even more stuff, making us even more uncomfortable than we were before; or they will join us because the only thing the religion had going for it was getting to hang out with us.

Another way to play for the other team without leaving your current religion is to accept that other doctrines have some merit to them. To many religions, this is salt in the wound, as they believe they have the only true access to the higher powers of the universe. While this ploy may not get you booted from the team, it'll definitely put your butt on the bench.

Rest On Your Laurels

This is my favorite of favorites of all-time favorites. Yes, I like it that much. And it's because it is so ironical (classical irony). So many religions speak of works that we do here on earth so that we can make it to the next level. Many of those works are good things that we do, but some religions actually have you do bad things, which, to them, are good things. But no matter, because either way, it's these "good" things that people grab on to. And this is F-bombing gold in so many religions.

Why? People get so wrapped up in the good

things they do that they lose sight of why they do them. We start to think that all those good deeds mean something. That those deeds are what will take us over the top. This is especially true for those who have yet to fully commit to a religion.

Man is a great guy. Man does all this good stuff for the people around him. Man has a good soul. Man never hurt anyone in his whole life. Man dies. Man is denied entry at the Pearly Gates. Now tell me that's not ironical!

And there are people all over the world like this. They walk around thinking that their being a great person is enough. But in the end, their being a great person is only good for everyone else. If I did have a story to tell about someone, I'd call him Gitt because it rhymes with 'won't commit.' One has to wonder if people who rest on their laurels are worse off than those who straddle that fence. I guess only the higher power knows for sure. But I do know that they are both F-bombing their religions. And I also know that for me, I'll leave the F-bombing religions to other folks. Like I said in the beginning, this branch of F-bombing scares the crap out of me! So rest on your laurels if you must, but I think I'll pass.

IN CLOSING

Now Good Luck to You (or bad luck to you as it may be)

I hope you have found this work to be not only helpful, but mildly entertaining as well. And I hope you took notes along the way so that you can easily go back and reference the techniques you want to try. F-bombing your life is serious business, but as I've shown, it is pretty easy to do. Some of you may already be so F-bombed that you didn't even realize it until after reading this book. Congratulations! You are just like me.

And one final thing to take away from this book is that you can either F-bomb your life or take the necessary steps to shield yourself, if that is indeed more your thing. I understand that F-bombing is not for everyone. We're all individuals seeking our own way. So who says that you want to be just like me? Do what feels right to you. But I know that in the end, you will not be able to stay away from the occasional F-bomb. Man has been F-bombing since time began, and quite frankly, I don't see an end to it any time soon.

Here's one last *almost true* story by/about a real-life F-bomber to hammer it home.

IN CLOSING

We will call him Rajah because it rhymes with 'ta-ta.'

There once was Rajah from Nantucket,
Who told his own life to just suck it.
Bewildered and confused,
He knew not what to do,
So he F-bombed it all for a bucket.
But this bucket was half full of wonder,
Unwilling to tear Rajah asunder.
So it hit him over the head
Leaving all he knew for dead
And Rajah started over down under.

ABOUT THE AUTHOR

Gregory Scott Kase lives and trains in Houston, TX. His workouts include dictionary lifting, mind bending, and running at the mouth, although no one ever listens. He has been called either incredibly brilliant or extremely stupid; the jury is still out, though, as the verdict of such deliberation will be life-altering for all those who know him, and especially for those who are related to him.

He is traditionally a writer of fiction, which has everyone who knows him utterly ticked off that he is not living in that world instead of theirs. He lives for research, even though his notepad is rarely welcome during those sensitive times when worlds crumble and heavens collide. But to Kase, there is much to be learned from two women fighting over the last pack of toilet paper at the dollar store.

Kase is a man of few words, mainly because he's never quite happy with the string of words that come to mind. But he does enjoy a good quote. One of his favorites is from Benjamin Franklin. It goes a little something like this: *Either write something worth reading or do something worth writing.* Kase has tried to use this himself but is often ridiculed for being too mean. He now sticks to his own thoughts which can be equally offensive.

www.ingramcontent.com/pod-product-compliance
Lightning Source LLC
Chambersburg PA
CBHW020002050426
42450CB00005B/280